Pr...

EATING *from the* SHEPHERD'S TABLE

"Dr. Cunningham provides a practical and applicable approach to understanding life's essentials from the Word of God. Much like his personal conviction, professionally, Dr. Cunningham shows a sincere desire to help God's people grasp the rich truths of the God of the Scriptures and the Scriptures disclosures about our divine God. This work helps us understand not only what God can do for us, but more importantly, what God expects from us."

–Rev. Guy A. Williams, Sr., D.Min., Pastor
Covenant Community Baptist Church
Silver Spring, Maryland

"Dr. Cunningham's dedication and devotion to studying the Word is only matched by his passion for preaching and teaching it to others. His messages have singlehandedly been a blessing to my life. ***The Shepherd's Table*** *has been well prepared and will provide nourishment for all who take a seat."*

–Jared Coles Carithers
Grad student, University of Maryland

"Dr. Cunningham is a genuine person who enthusiastically delivers messages that exemplify his love for the Lord and all people. He labors before the Lord to increase his understanding and delivery of God's unwavering "fresh words" of encouragement and praise that he plainly articulates to anyone he encounters in everyday life and to his congregation. Dr. Cunningham perseveres through his kind, yet exuberant, witty spirit that clearly edifies God's promises and plan for your life."

–Mrs. Regina Byrd
Trustee Board Member, Hear the Word Bible Church

"I would strongly recommend reading this book by Dr. Thomas E. Cunningham. Thomas is a man of great character and exemplifies great leadership skills and a mastery of communication. He has successfully navigated a ministry from its infancy to a powerful hallmark in the community."

–Bishop Kevin Gresham Sr. Pastor
Greater Saint John Cathedral
Upper Marlboro, Maryland

"Dr. Cunningham has been my dear friend for over 20 years and this book demonstrates his untiring heart for God and His Word! "Heart gripping" is what I think of when I read this devotional! The reader will not only find this to be refreshing to their perspective, but it will also restore life's focus and priority on this Christian journey."

–Rev. Jeffrey Allen, Retired Navy Veteran

To: Michelle

EATING *from the* SHEPHERD'S TABLE

"Meet me at the table"

Thomas E Cunningham

Jn 10:27

Thomas E. Cunningham

EATING *from the* SHEPHERD'S TABLE

Published by Exodus Christian Book Publishing
www.exoduschristianbookpublishing.com

ISBN: 9781793084392

Editing services by ChristianEditingServices.com

Book cover design and interior layout by Kristine Cotterman, Exodus Design Studio, www.exodusdesign.com

For more information about the book and author,
visit www.shepherdstablebook.com

This book is dedicated to

my love and heartbeat, Candace (Pretty).

You have encouraged me in so many ways to keep sharing those things that will touch the souls of many. Thank you for being my best friend and wife.

To Daria (Cupcake), Jasmine, and Jared … may your dad's life as a sheep of the Great Shepherd serve as an added witness for you of the grace and mercy of our Lord Jesus Christ.

Finally, this book is dedicated to all those who have faced traumas and trials in life, yet continue to search for and chase the will of the Lord. He is speaking. Let us all hear His voice.

Contents

1.	God's Going to Let My Prayer Go Public	1
2.	Don't Get Infected with Fear	7
3.	Lord, Keep Me in Check	13
4.	God Is Not in Trouble!	19
5.	From Forgiven to Forgiving	25
6.	Lord, Open My Eyes and Close Their Mouths	31
7.	I Declare War	37
8.	What Do You Want?	43
9.	This Was My Last Weak!	49
10.	Don't Take in What God Said Keep Out	55
11.	By His Hands	61
12.	You're Looking at the Results of Grace and Mercy	67
13.	A Purpose in My Pain	73
14.	Full of Activity but Bearing No Fruit	79
15.	Escaping Strife's Traps	85
16.	Wait	91
17.	The Danger of Almost	97
18.	When the Enemy Comes	103
19.	From Fire to Function	109
20.	Standing on the Promises, Not the Premises	115
21.	What to Expect When You Are Expecting	121

22.	The Devil is a Liar, I Know the Truth	127
23.	Dig Wherever You Are Asked to Dwell	133
24.	Turning Back Is Not the Way Forward	139
25.	Lord, You Handle It!	145
26.	When Your Enemies Are Counting on the Lions, You Count on God	153
27.	When Faith Is Attacked by Doubt	161
28.	I Am Convinced!	167
29.	When It Sits at the Tip of the Tongue	173
30.	The Pressure of Pride	179
31.	It's Behind Me Now	187

Foreword

It is my esteemed pleasure to introduce Dr. Thomas E. Cunningham, who happens to be my eldest brother. Growing up as one of seven siblings, I always attended church, and this activity was a top priority in the household. Many attributes were also instilled in me during my upbringing, and while some were valuable, others were not as beneficial. Whether you are a new seeker in Christ or looking for purpose or one who already knows their purpose, but seeking to strengthen your walk in the Lord, there is something in this book for you.

I was elated when I learned that Dr. Cunningham's first project would include sermon excerpts from his personal sermon library. Dr. Cunningham's words, his passion, and love for Jesus Christ is contagious. As a reader, not only will your life be enriched, but I truly believe that you will also be encouraged and your soul will be overwhelmingly blessed. This is a breakthrough devotional book that will prove to be timeless, providing a link between hearing the voice of the Lord and life application for all readers.

Within the covers of this book, you will find a body of passionate, edifying, thought-provoking, and challenging devotions. In your first reading, you will begin to notice many life applications that will undoubtedly feed your soul and prove how relevant to your daily life. It is not simply a collection of messages and spiritual strategies, but is designed to build understanding for a firmer and infallible Christian walk. Certainly, anyone can develop a random collection of lessons, but finding lesson that will challenge the reader to dig deeper into their spiritual quest is indeed rare.

I personally enjoyed the opportunity to have read and even apply many of these devotions to my own life, and this has enabled me to grow exponentially in my spiritual walk with the

Lord. I have learned during my own time of meditation, that it is essential to be still and seek the voice of God. This book is not only instructional, but it is also testimonial, and a reader can use the teachings to seek God. It unfolds an amazing view of humility when it comes to the Christian's position in Christ.

As a professional photographer and author myself of several well-renowned books, including Crowns, Portraits of Black Women in Church Hats (foreword by Maya Angelou), Spirit of Harlem, Queens, and Jewels I have been blessed to experience great success. Moreover, I have had a theatrical adaptation of Crowns playing to sold-out audiences across the U.S. and Canada, and currently, the play is still on tour. Therefore, I am profoundly aware of the impact that written words can have on a reader's life.

I am currently under Dr. Cunningham's tutelage, a 'sheep' at Hear the Word Bible Church. Hence, I can truly attest to his personal devotion and commitment to the Lord. Not all devotional books are the same, and you will indisputably observe this from the Author's writings. Dr. Cunningham grips the heart of the believer with the incredible vision of a sheep in the presence of a shepherd. To get the news, you have to understand the story, and this book needs to be in the hands of those who are looking forward to the next level of hearing the voice of the Lord.

Michael Cunningham

(Author, Professional Photographer, Founder and Executive Director of Urban Shutterbugs, a nonprofit organization teaching the fine art of photography to youth)

Acknowledgments

This book developed out of a series of sermons that I was blessed to minister over the years. I am eternally grateful to God who has brought my life and heart into a Shepherd/sheep relationship with my Savior and Lord Jesus Christ. Thanks to my book designer and editing team. My unbroken appreciation goes to my wife, Candace, for all of the invaluable laboring, never-ending support, and help in bringing all my research together. I want to extend a sincere thank you to Juanita, my sis, for her assistance and ideas. To Dennis and Patricia (father/mother) and to Hear The Word Bible Church, I am forever grateful for your continual prayers and support.

Introduction

Growing up in a home where attending church was required, I wasn't guaranteed salvation or a relationship with Christ, but it did teach me who was controlling my life until such time as I could make a personal decision to follow the Lord. I owe the good, early direction to my father and mother, who answered their own callings as minister (dad) and evangelist (mom) of the gospel of Jesus Christ.

I am a person who tries to respond in original ways that are "outside the box." I have always been in awe of the powers of prayer, observation, wisdom, and wisdom's translation into action. We live in a civilization that is starving and indeed suffering from the lack of all four of these sacred practices.

During my quiet times, I have wandered off and pondered what the views of animals might be who, like us, were created by God. How are they communicating thanks to Him for being the provider and caretaker?

Some of my best contemplations on life occur in the early mornings. That's when the meditative moment that inspired this devotional book began for me. In an attempt to maximize my day, I often sit on my back patio, using the time to study, listen, and wonder as I read the book of Psalms.

I have always been a bird lover, and owning a few birds in my life, I experienced the interesting perspective of being their nurturer: the hand that fed and provided shelter to a creature placed under my care. I contemplated that experience one morning while reading the Twenty-Third Psalm. "The Lord is my shepherd. I shall not want," says the psalmist, comparing God to a shepherd lovingly tending his sheep. The psalm reveals David's firsthand experience as a sheep herder, and the purpose and attention that are needed to lead and protect a flock. This experience birthed his own understanding and appreciation of God as the Great Shepherd of his life.

David, a shepherd boy, began to see what life was about and who he was in the eyes of the Lord. Myself being one who seeks guidance, patience, and perseverance, I am sometimes perplexed, as David at times was, over the works and sovereignty of an all-knowing, all-loving God. But David saw through to life's purpose. Although there were probably times when he could not comprehend the purpose behind life's upheavals and challenges, he nevertheless found comfort, like a sheep, in the corrections of the rod, knowing God was directing his every step.

I am confident there were more things that David could have penned that have never been shared. I wondered about those precious, unheard, hidden thoughts and prayers. So, I thought (with my spiritual imagination): what if a sheep were given an intimate position in the field of the Lord, lying right beside the Shepherd's feet at His table, quietly listening while He spoke to those of old? Those who have gone before us, enduring life's many trials and bringing their questions and fears from the field to discuss while eating around that table. What would that conversation be like, and what could I take away from it and apply to my own life?

I am reminded of a biblical passage—Matthew 15:27-28—where the distraught woman cries, "Yes, Lord, but even the dogs eat the crumbs that fall from their master's table." Then Jesus answers her, "O woman, great is your faith! Be it done for you as you desire." And her daughter is instantly healed.

What a bold request and expectation from that woman! She was willing to receive whatever Jesus decided to hand her or let fall. We can glean a precious nugget of wisdom from that passage: that the same ingredients in the loaf are also in the crumbs. It's a matter of spiritual perspective.

My quest, in creating this 31-day devotional book, was to pull away from the table spiritual food that can be utilized in our everyday life. I started collecting excerpts from sermons I'd ministered over the years. How would it sound, I wondered, if a sheep could talk about what had been discussed around the Good Shepherd's table? How would that translate for us to continue our Christian journey through this path of life?

In order to get the most out of these readings, I suggest that you view yourself as that humble sheep. The day of grazing has ended, the sun is setting, and calmness has settled down over the flock. You've returned from a day of gleaning green pastures beside still waters, experiencing at times the threats against your peace from ravenous wolves or other predators. Picture yourself having this awe-inspiring opportunity to listen to the words being spoken by your Shepherd at His table.

It is amazing how we can hear the same words again and again, yet each time take away new insights and applications, depending on where we are in our lives. It is my sincere prayer that each day's devotion followed by a sheep's prayer may bring you closer to God and allow you to view yourself as one out of many that were granted this astounding position. As you begin with prayer, come expecting to receive something from the table. I pray that the Lord will speak and encourage your heart as you sit in and listen.

"Oh that my words were now written! Oh that they were printed in a book." (Job 19:23)

Thomas E. Cunningham

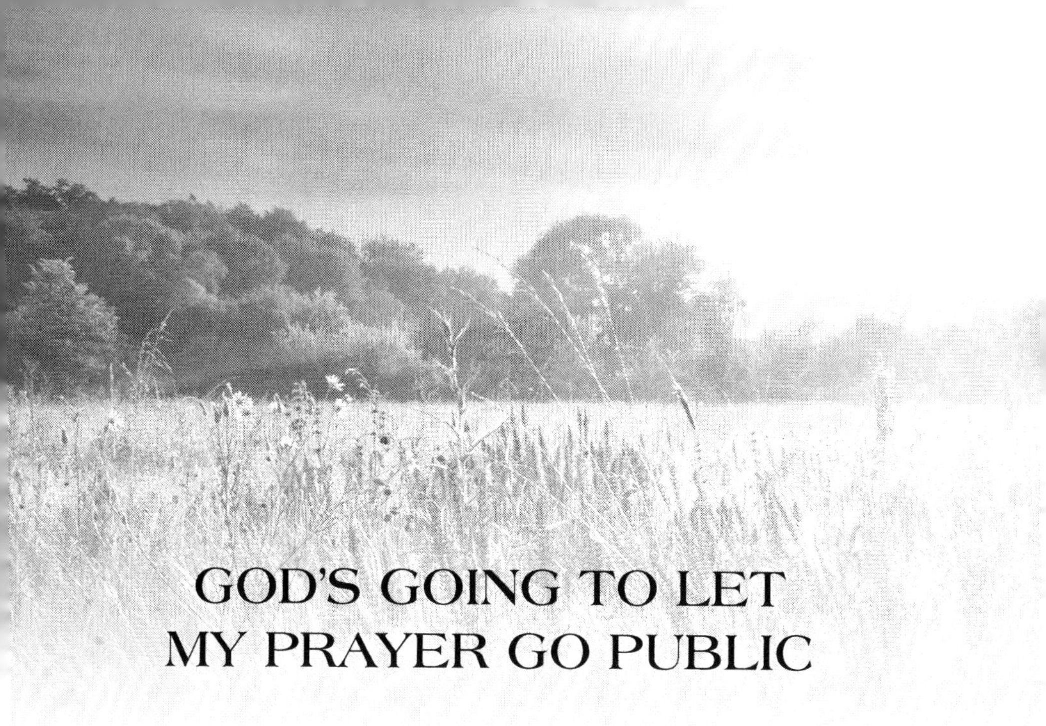

GOD'S GOING TO LET MY PRAYER GO PUBLIC

"But when you pray, go into your room and shut the door
and pray to your Father who is in secret.
And your Father who sees in secret
will reward you."
(Matthew 6:6)

"The greatest tragedy of life is not unanswered prayer, but unoffered prayer." — F.B. Meyer[1]

Day 1

THE TABLE TALK

Everyone has a special place to relax and do some of their favorite things, but how many of us have a special place where we meet with our Father in prayer? This place should be somewhere that allows us to shut everything and everyone out, a place where we can pray freely and openly to God. If we are truly seeking intimacy with our Father, we must have privacy—a sacred sanctuary where God can meet us. Our prayer "closet" should be free from distractions, interruptions, and outside of the hearing of others.

The enemy knows how critical our prayers can be, so he tries to have us abandon the very idea of seeking God in prayer. If he cannot keep us from praying, he attempts to discourage us with such tactics as doubt and anxiety. When what we have prayed for does not happen right away, we may begin to think that our prayers are unanswered or futile.

Prayer is a highly-esteemed privilege extended by God to believers. Our motivation for praying should not be to be known as a praying person but to know our Father in heaven. Jesus taught that we should go into our rooms and shut the door to pray so that no one will praise us and our reward will be from the Father instead. Jesus called those who liked to be heard and seen praying "hypocrites," who have already received their reward through men's praise. Our quiet prayers, directed to God and not to be heard by those around us, allow us to reap spiritual blessings. Jesus also taught against babbling and vain repetitions, thinking that we will be heard because we use many words. God is not impressed by our earnestness in prayer, nor does He hear us because we pray earnestly with numerous or fancy words. He hears us solely on the basis of redemption.

Prayer should be our response to the grace and mercy God has extended to us. We often abuse this privilege by using it to give God information, to solicit more blessings or benefits, or to demand our rights. Our prayers should not be forced conversations merely pushed by the pressures of our desires or situations. We should not be praying to pull God toward our will, but we should seek to align our will with His. Often we pray to get hold of the answer, but we should be praying to get hold of God. Our eyes should be focused on Him, not our difficulties. God does not respond to our prayers. He responds to us. We must recognize that our need for God is not partial, but total—requiring an attitude of dependency. When we humbly and truthfully seek God we willingly wait on His answer because we know it will always end in thanksgiving, triumph, and praise.

His Word tells us that all of God's promises are yes and amen unto the glory of God (2 Corinthians 1:20). Through our amen to the Word of God, we confirm His words and invoke the fulfillment of His promises in our lives. Through our private fellowship with God we receive public benefit. If we pray to the Lord in secret, He shall reward us publicly.

When we humbly and truthfully seek God we willingly wait on His answer because we know it will always end in thanksgiving, triumph, and praise.

Our Lord Jesus stressed the hypocrisy of those who prayed, gave offerings, or did charitable acts in front of others—in order to elevate themselves and draw praise from their community. As Matthew 6:6 makes clear, however, God is moved by private prayer, not prayers for show but those that spring from faith. He is always with us, and when we pray to Him in private He sees our sincere belief. Even though God tells us He is with those who gather together to worship and pray (Matthew 18:20), which is the foundation of the religious community and the church, private prayer also has its time. When we seek God's grace in solitude we are not alone, for He is with us.

A SHEEP'S REQUEST

Heavenly Father, thank You for the privilege to come to You in prayer. Sometimes it may seem as if You fail to hear me and that my prayers are not being answered. Teach me to learn to wait on You knowing that You will answer and fulfill Your promises to me according to Your wisdom and will. Amen.

DON'T GET INFECTED WITH FEAR

"But now for a brief moment favor has been shown by the Lord our God, to leave us a remnant and to give us a secure hold within his holy place, that our God may brighten our eyes and grant us a little reviving in our slavery" (v. 8).
(Ezra 9:1–15)

"I will not fear, for you are ever with me,
and you will never leave me to face my perils alone."
— Thomas Merton[2]

Day 2

THE TABLE TALK

Have you ever noticed how easy it is for many to look as if they are faithful until faith is actually required? Often, our exterior is decorated in faith bearing a remarkable similarity to someone who has true faith, but in reality we live in fear. Fear is merely fake faith. Fear is faith against God. If we lack of concentration, if we cannot focus on studying the Word, our faith crumbles and fear settles in our hearts. What would our lives and conversations be like if we had no fear? When we have no fear we are simply saying that this problem or situation is not in our hands—it belongs to God.

The enemy is constantly seeking us out, making us part of his agenda because of what he knows God has placed inside of us. God has marked us as His own, meaning we are anointed, appointed, and have favor and blessing upon our lives. Because of this, the enemy sees us as targets and plots to attack the work of God in our lives. We pose a direct threat to him but have no need to fear because God has not given us the spirit of fear. We have power through Christ Jesus to overcome the enemy. When we have no fear, we reveal by our faith that we are confident he will be destroyed.

The Holy Spirit has to constantly remind us of who we are in Christ and what He has been done for us. We cannot allow worry to paralyze us into inactivity, because faith is always on the move, and a moving target is hard to hit. The truly faithful stop to pray and gather what they need for the enemy's next attack before moving on. If we permit him to seize us with anxiety long enough to terrorize us, then he will have an open door to dismantle our faith.

The Holy Spirit has to constantly remind us of who we are in Christ and what He has been done for us.

In our passage today we see that the Israelites disobeyed God's command against intermingling with the Hittites (whose name, by the way, means "sons of terror"). Instead of continuing to walk in faith, they began to engage in the detestable practices of non-believers. When we mismanage our faith, the fight with the enemy becomes misdirected and our connection with the Lord becomes contaminated. The day we choose to intermingle with the enemy is the day we choose fear. When fear sets in we start to give in. We either have strong faith and weak fear or strong fear and weak faith, but we cannot have both.

Jesus, however, gave us a resolution to Ezra's dilemma in the form of the Great Commission (Matt 28:16–20), wherein we are instructed to seek out non-believers, not to be tainted by them but to spread God's glory to them. This demonstrates the strength of our faith in front of our enemies by approaching them with the offer of faith in the one true God, so that they may turn from wickedness and enjoy His blessings.

A SHEEP'S REQUEST

Heavenly Father, help me to run the race I was born to win. In Christ Jesus I am not a victim but a victor. I will not be afraid of what the enemy can do to me, for You have called me out of bondage. I will not become paralyzed by fear but will move forward in faith as You enable me to withstand the enemy's attacks. My hope, my trust, my faith is in You. Amen.

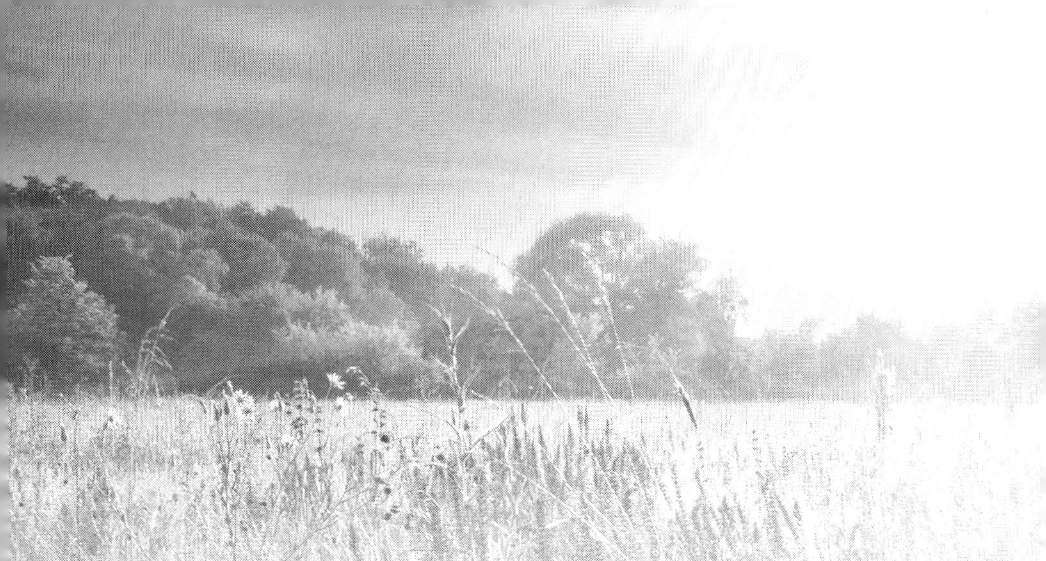

LORD, KEEP ME IN CHECK

"And he said, 'Behold, I am making a covenant.
Before all your people I will do marvels,
such as have not been created in all the earth or in any nation.
And all the people among whom you are shall see
the work of the Lord, for it is an awesome thing
that I will do with you'" (v. 10).
(Exodus 34:10–17)

"Chastisement is designed for our good, to promote our highest interests. Look beyond the rod to the All-wise hand that wields it!"
— A.W. Pink[3]

Day 3

THE TABLE TALK

Every child of God needs two things: faithful warnings and caring encouragements. The Lord, in His infinite wisdom and care, provides us with both. His faithful warnings curb our sinful drifts and propensities, and His caring encouragements flow with spiritual grace, so that we may accomplish what He has called us to do.

We must recognize the Lord's hand daily and surrender to Him in our lives. His promises are not made to the work but to the worker, not for the worker's own sake but for the sake of Jesus Christ. Erwin Lutzer said, "Spiritual surgery is more painful than physical surgery. God doesn't use an anesthetic; He doesn't do His work while we are asleep. . . . But when He performs such 'heart operations,' His children are wide awake."[4] God wants us to see what He is doing in our lives. Although we will experience some pain in the process, it's not enough pain to kill us, only enough to sustain us.

The enemy will be quick to see if we continue to stand on what we have learned. He causes the attraction of "don't touch" or "don't do this or that" to appear as an attack on our freedom, as if God were trying to limit us or keep us from enjoying life. He attempts to pressure our flesh into viewing God's warnings as interfering with the fulfilling our desires. He seeks to break down our resistance to see if we are truly committed to the Lord. You see, the enemy already knows the answers found in God's Word, but how much of it do we really know?

We must recognize the Lord's hand daily and surrender to Him in our lives. His promises are not made to the work but to the worker . . .

During trials and temptations do we become agitated by the words God has spoken or are we able to recognize that they are God's caring encouragement to keep us from falling prey to the enemy's schemes? The greatest possibility for rebellion comes when we believe the lies that the enemy presents as truth. We become distracted and our attention is diverted. We become enticed by a false, undisciplined lifestyle just as the Israelites did when they became ensnared by comparing themselves with the Perizzites, despite the Lord warning them not only to avoid these heretics but also to actively reject their idols and false worship.

This should be a familiar refrain, given the number of times the Lord has warned us to not become entangled, to avoid something, or to let something go—yet we willfully disobey Him. Walking in the way of righteousness is hard, because such a path may not yield the immediate material benefits that people crave. Nevertheless, we must believe that God's faithful warnings, caring encouragements, and jealousy all spring from His passion to protect us and steer the purpose of our lives. He has so much He wants to do for us that He jealously desires our wholehearted devotion. Why would we want to go back to the bondage of material cravings and false idols? We will not be free *from* something without being free *for* something else. We must be free from bondage by allowing the Holy Spirit to help us master our own desires and actions in order to be free for Him and the work that He has for us. We must live under the Holy Spirit's control in order to live a controlled life. Only His love can break the chains that bind us, set us free, and give us life (for He is life) now and forever!

A SHEEP'S REQUEST

Heavenly Father, thank You for the freedom I have in You. I am grateful that I no longer have to remain bound by the lies of the enemy. I am set free by Your warnings and encouragement. Help me to heed to Your Word and not become entangled in the false freedom this world has to offer. Teach me to live a disciplined life so that Your will may be fulfilled in me. You have set me free by Your love, passion, and protection. Amen.

GOD IS NOT IN TROUBLE!

"He said, "Do not be afraid, for those who are with us are more than those who are with them"' (v. 16).
(2 Kings 6:8–17)

"A God wise enough to create me and the world I live in is wise enough to watch out for me."
— Philip Yancey[5]

Day 4

THE TABLE TALK

As servants of the Lord we will be exposed to many conflicts, oppositions, and dangers throughout our lifetime, until the will and purpose of God in our lives has been completed. When we face these challenges, our instinct is to want to avoid or somehow change the situation, but then we realize that we can do neither and must accept what God allows. Fear often sets in and cripples us, causing us to spiral into a vortex of worry. We begin to fuel our fear with the thoughts of what might be or what we imagine could be. But if we are in Christ and cling to Him by faith, we have no need to be anxious or afraid. We tend to fear our issues more than we fear our Lord because we see them as larger and more powerful than He is.

In our passage today, Elisha was surrounded by the whole Syrian army who was determined to kill him. Elisha's servant began to panic and asked, "What shall we do," realizing that the Syrians were great in number. This is what the servant saw with his natural eyes. Elisha had to remind him there was no need to fear. He knew that in spite of the large army headed towards them they had the majority because they were on the Lord's side. Their enemies were like dust compared to the strength of the Almighty! The Syrian army was not aware, but they were vastly outnumbered. Elisha had but to pray and ask the Lord to strike them with blindness, and suddenly the entire army went blind. His simple faith in an all-powerful God reduced a seemingly unstoppable foe to nothing. We may not have experienced a physical army rising up against us like the prophet Elisha, but we do face enemies in the form of spiritual powers that inspire anxiety and fear, attempting to shake our faith and ultimately destroy us. These spiritual powers that oppose us today are just as dangerous as the Syrian army that surrounded Elisha. It is easy for us to quickly feel outnumbered. Sometimes, we too become blinded by what we see in the natural.

We become blinded by what we see in the natural. Physical sight only allows us to see what is happening; spiritual vision allows us to see what will happen. Sight causes us to look at the predicament; vision helps us to see the potential. Sight looks at the present; vision holds onto the promises of God. Our natural sight only allows us to see the problem, but our spiritual sight allows us to see the protection. In God, we have the ability to see the problem and solution at the same time. Nothing is too big for God to handle, and nothing is too small to escape His attention. Nothing that happens in our lives catches God by surprise. His power is manifested in our weakness. We are in His protective custody. We do not have to wonder or worry about whether God can take care of our situations.

Sight causes us to look at the predicament;
vision helps us to see the potential.

Satan wants us to feel alone and that the odds are stacked against us. He attempts to get us to rely on our own strength. We must realize that by faith, with God on our side no one can be against us—the enemy will not prevail. We have no need to fear or panic. No matter the crisis, no matter the dark days, no matter the trials, and no matter the disappointments—rest assured, God is not in trouble! When others work against us, as the king of Aram did against God's prophet Elijah, God will reveal that we are protected with the strength of horses and chariots of fire through our faith.

A SHEEP'S REQUEST

Heavenly Father, please help me to not view my problems as bigger than You! Remove fear and doubt from my heart so that I will not worry about what I see in front of me, but instead learn to become sure of what I hope for despite what I see. Lord, You are my light and my salvation. You are the strength of my life, so I do not have to be afraid. I place my trust in You, knowing that You have everything in control! Enlighten my challengers and keep me safe all my days. Amen.

FROM FORGIVEN TO FORGIVING

"It was fitting to celebrate and be glad,
for this your brother was dead, and is alive;
he was lost, and is found" (v. 32).
(Luke 15:11–32)

"To be a Christian means to forgive the inexcusable because God has forgiven the inexcusable in you."
— *C.S. Lewis*[6]

Day 5

THE TABLE TALK

All of us have at some time or another been wounded by the mistreatment, mistakes, injustices, and even betrayals of other people. We can find it difficult to forgive and instead begin to rehearse the pain we've experienced over and over in our minds. This only serves to nurse our wounds and does not allow for healing. Medical studies have shown that unforgiveness directly correlates to certain illnesses in our body. God has designed our bodies to eject contaminants, but when we hold onto grudges, anger, and unforgiveness we contaminate our heart, mind, body, and soul.

If someone hurts us and seeks to be forgiven we are to fully forgive them. The Lord's prayer teaches us to forgive those who trespass against us, even as we ask God to forgive our trespasses. The Lord has forgiven us of the worst of sins, so we are to forgive the worst of sins done unto us. Don't confuse forgiveness with forgetting. God does not expect us to forget, approve, or excuse the behavior of those who hurt us. He does, however, require us to forgive one another. The act of forgiving will never make a wrong right, and God is the only one who can remove the pain of being hurt. John R. Rice says, "By God's grace, a Christian can so forgive that every memory brings not bitterness but a sweet sense of peace without any rancor or bitterness whatever."[7] Forgiving those who sin against us helps us to develop more of the character of Christ within us.

Jesus's death on the cross, forgiving us of all sins past, present, and future, is the greatest act of forgiveness ever. Even in our scripture passage today, the Lord gives us another great example of forgiveness through the parable of the lost son. The lost son's father welcomed him home with open arms even after he had selfishly hurt and disrespected him when he left him to seek his fortune away from his family. The father clearly had not forgotten what his son had done, but he forgave him and opened the door for reconciliation to begin. If we want to be forgiven by our heavenly Father, we must likewise forgive one another.

Forgiveness is resting your case in the hands of the Lord, not in the offender. When we refuse to forgive, we are trying that person's case in our own courtroom, which means we have not turned it over to God. Our hurt is legitimate, but God will not judge the case as long as we are holding on to the files of records of what has been done to us. The Bible teaches us that vengeance belongs to the Lord alone.

Forgiveness is resting your case in the hands of the Lord, not in the offender.

If we don't rest our case and let the Lord handle it, we will become imprisoned by our own bitterness. Forgiveness always seems easy when we need it and hard when we need to give it. Fret not, my brother, my sister. God always has a way of helping us to forgive what we cannot forget and turning what we cannot forget into a testimony!

A SHEEP'S REQUEST

Heavenly Father, please forgive me for my transgressions and offenses against You and others. Help me to forgive others as You have forgiven me. Thank You for the power to keep going even when it's hard to forget. You have released me. You have set me free. No more added sickness or worry. The chains of unforgiveness are falling off! Amen.

LORD, OPEN MY EYES AND CLOSE THEIR MOUTHS

"And Jesus said to him,
'What do you want me to do for you?'
And the blind man said to him,
'Rabbi, let me recover my sight'" (v. 51).
(Mark 10:46–52)

*"However many blessings we expect from God,
His infinite liberality will always exceed
all our wishes and our thoughts."
— John Calvin*[8]

Day 6

THE TABLE TALK

It is amazing how two people can be involved in the same situation yet have very different perceptions about what happened. One of the major contributing factors in differing individual perceptions is each person's handle on life—how one views circumstances, one's emotional and physical feelings at the time, and his or her spiritual journey with the Lord. These dynamics directly impact how one navigates and responds to life's challenges and opportunities.

If we are bound to material or carnal desires and reject God's insight, our responses will be ruled by our senses and emotions. What we think and do will be controlled by sin and natural circumstances. Life and peace come when we are spiritually centered. We must be so in tune with God that we are willing to become blind—blind to our pride and earthly, carnal mindset. Only then will we be able to see with our hearts what God wants to show us. Only then will He reveal to us His hand at work in our difficult struggles.

According to Helen Keller, it is "better to be blind and see with your heart than to have two good eyes and see nothing."[9] The key to spiritual focus is to see not only what we see with our eyes, but also to ask the Lord to reveal to us what we may miss through our other senses. Although the people near Jericho told blind Bartimaeus, a beggar, to "hold his peace" and stop beseeching Jesus for aid, he kept crying out. He was aware of his own faith and temporal condition. He was not about to allow anyone to stop him from *seeing* what the Lord would do to help him.

Sometimes the Lord will not let you see so that you can hear Him. Bartimaeus was a blind beggar sitting beside the highway asking for alms. He could not *see* Jesus coming, but he *heard* that Jesus was walking by. He was aware of all that Jesus had been teaching and doing. He had time to make up his mind about what Jesus may have done for others and what He could do for him. Although he could not see Jesus or the miracles He wrought, he believed everything he had heard. We must be like this beggar and remember that we walk by faith and not by sight. We look not at the things which are seen, but at the things which are not seen. For the things seen are temporal, and the Bible tells us that we are blessed if we have not seen and yet believe. We may not always know the where, the when, or the how, but we do believe the Who!

We must be so in tune with God that we are willing to become blind—blind to our pride and earthly, carnal mindset.

Sometimes the Lord will not let you see so that you can ask. The beggar asked the Lord for a specific mercy. "Rabbi, let me recover my sight" (v. 51). In order to receive his sight, he had to be willing to throw away his support. He cast aside his garment (v. 50), appealed to Jesus, and immediately received his sight. "Go your way; your faith has made you well" (v. 52).

Sometimes the Lord will not let you see so that you can see. Because Bartimaeus was willing to trust God, he received his sight, and as a result he followed Jesus. It's our *faith* in God, not faith in our own faith, that counts. Sight comes from the Master Teacher—God Himself! The disciples and others were not able to see what Bartimaeus saw, because he was relying on his faith in Jesus. Because of his ability to see by faith, he received his physical sight and increased his spiritual sight. Of course, everyone was amazed and left speechless at the miracle Jesus performed. The Lord opened a man's eyes and simultaneously closed the mouths of those around him!

A SHEEP'S REQUEST

Heavenly Father, grant me a fresh sight of Your power, favor, and will. Open my heart as well as my eyes so that I can see. Close the mouths of non-believers who maintain that grace will never happen for me, and keep me covered as I place my unquestioning faith in You! Amen.

I DECLARE WAR

"And when the Lord your God gives them over to you, and you defeat them, then you must devote them to complete destruction. You shall make no covenant with them and show no mercy to them" (v. 2).
(Deuteronomy 7:1–9)

"Without God we cannot,
and without us God will not."
— Augustine[10]

Day 7

THE TABLE TALK

Life has its share of battles, even though the war itself has already been won through the sacrifice of the Lamb of God. As long as we delight in the law of the Lord, we will have conflict. Our human nature fights against the changes produced by faith. We must consider whether we fight the battles that we pick or the ones chosen for us. If we choose our own battles, we will gain nothing spiritually and find ourselves battle fatigued. We will become worn out because our response will be from the flesh. We will try to fight these battles in our own strength instead of in the strength of the Lord.

Too often we try to make God the champion of our cause rather than seeking His work.

Sometimes our weariness also comes from fighting the wrong battles. We can end up fighting ourselves instead of our real enemy, because we become entangled in the battle itself. Alternatively, when we engage in battles chosen for us by the Lord, we grow exponentially, because we recognize that in order to fight our formidable foes, we must employ God's strength. Too often we try to make God the champion of our cause rather than seeking His work. Our hearts must be fixed firmly on what we will or will not do before we encounter the battle. Therefore, we must allow the Lord to prepare our hearts so that we will become strong in our knowledge of God's strength.

The Lord always provides us with time to prepare for the battles He chooses, but we must use that time wisely. We cannot ignore or minimize the preparation season needed to make us victorious. If we do not settle the battle in our hearts and minds before the fight, we will be overcome by our own thoughts and feelings. We must remind ourselves that Paul said, "Nay, in all these things we are more than conquerors through him that loved us" (Romans 8:37 KJV). Whenever we discover and heed the will of God, therein we will find our weapons for warfare.

The enemy attacks us because of our faith in Christ Jesus. His goal is to keep us from knowing what we have so that he can sell us what we do not need. The enemy is prepared to do anything to anybody as long as he can get somebody to do something. Just as the enemy convinced the Israelites to intermingle with the nations, he attempts to get us to believe and act in opposition to what God commands.

Anytime someone becomes a new creature in Christ and moves from being contaminated to being connected, they will have conflict.

Anytime someone becomes a new creature in Christ and moves from being contaminated to being connected, they will have conflict. Wherever innocence is found the enemy will attack, not because we are innocent but because of the Holy Spirit working through us. Satan is not concerned with attacking us in the hidden areas of our lives because he knows he can easily defeat us where we are vulnerable. This is why the Lord requires us, as He did the Israelites, to completely destroy those areas in our lives that will interfere with our conquering and possessing the land.

When we refuse to obey what the Lord tells us, we will suffer the consequences of our disobedience and jeopardize our victory. In our waywardness and rebellion, we extend our battles—we delay our ability to enjoy what God has prepared for us. God has given us an inheritance to enjoy in Christ Jesus that surpasses what we are able to imagine. The Lord desires us to reach immeasurable depths and heights. All that we can think or desire is ours through the covenant God has made with us. Let us not forfeit our inheritance of earthly and heavenly treasures by battling on our own.

The Lord wants us to claim a land and works of justice by overcoming worldly challenges. If we battle His way, we will see the battle won in advance! God sends us out prepared to fight from a winning position. When the Lord sets up the battle, our job is simply to possess and claim the land! You have to conquer in order to claim!

A SHEEP'S REQUEST

Heavenly Father, forgive me for choosing my own battles. I pray for wisdom to not become entangled with battles that You have not chosen for me. Increase my knowledge and understanding of who You are so that I may be prepared for the battles that come my way. In You my battles are already won! Amen.

WHAT DO YOU WANT?

"Jesus turned and saw them following and said to them, 'What are you seeking?' And they said to him, 'Rabbi' (which means Teacher), 'where are you staying?'" (v. 38).
(John 1:35–39)

"Seek not to understand that you may believe, but believe that you may understand."
— Augustine[11]

Day 8

THE TABLE TALK

Have you ever thought about what you want? Most of us have, but often we focus on material things. It is impossible to move forward when we cannot admit to what we truly desire. Sometimes what we say we want does not line up with our actions or with what is truly in our hearts. Our treasure lies in our hearts, and God reads the expressions of our hearts the same way we read the expressions on faces. What expressions are our hearts showing Him today?

Metaphorically, the heart is where our faith, deepest imaginations, and decisions are seated. The direction of the heart controls what we love and desire the most. Some say desire is a better measure of one's character than behavior. Of all our desires in life, there should be one concrete desire serving as the springboard for all the others: our desire for Christ. If we choose to set and fix our hearts on Jesus and commit to following His life, He will supply all of our needs and grant our desires according to His will. Following Christ is the only way to see "God results" in our lives.

***We do not seek God because He is lost,
but we seek Him because we are lost without Him.***

We cannot just follow Him halfway. We must decide to choose Him over earthly temptations. It is impossible to serve two masters; whatever we choose also chooses us. Ultimately, we become a product of our desires and choices. Jesus asked His disciples a deceptively simple question, "What are you looking for?" or "Why are you following me?" This is the fundamental question Jesus asks of all of us: *"What do we seek?"* The disciples asked Jesus where He was going to stay, which in this context does not simply mean for one night but in essence where Jesus would permanently abide. He responded, "Come and you will see," which was an invitation to the disciples as well as an invitation to us to approach Jesus with the openness to see Him through the eyes of faith.

Human beings were created for relationship with God, and if we do not seek Him, how will we know Him and understand our purpose or His great love? God does not push Himself upon us, but He desires relationship with us and longs for us. Once we have experienced a portion of who God is, our desire to know Him should increase all the more. We do not seek God because He is lost, but we seek Him because we are lost without Him. We seek God because He has invited us to seek Him, so that we may more deeply and profoundly understand Him. Knowing God is an honor and privilege, and we are responsible to hunger and thirst after Him.

Seeking the Lord means seeking His presence continually! Jeremiah 29:13 tells us that if we seek Him with our whole heart we will find Him. Certainly, God is always present with us, but we can become neglectful of Him, giving Him no thought and failing to trust in Him. Thus His presence becomes hidden behind our fears and carnal desires. "Set your minds on things that are above, not on things that are on earth" (Colossians 3:2). We must not allow our minds to coast because seeking God requires conscious effort. God shows Himself to us in many ways—through the heavens, through His Word, and even in the grace that He has extended to us. It is imperative that we do not allow our hearts and minds to be distorted or blinded by our own worldly yearnings to the extent that they override our passion for seeking the Lord.

How many times have you struggled with a problem and drawn your conclusion before the search? There will always be a price to pay in pressing to know the Lord, but there is also a priceless result when we follow Him. Seeking Jesus is the only search where failure is impossible, for in doing so our seeking will always be crowned with finding. It is good for us to be where Christ is. We must come with a determined resolve to be firm and constant, solid and steadfast that we may obtain His favor and eternal life. The more we seek Him, the more He transforms us and the more our desires conform to His will. God promises to reveal Himself to those who seek Him, and that alone is our utmost reward.

A SHEEP'S REQUEST

Heavenly Father, my heart chooses You. May the expressions of my heart be pleasing to You. I seek You from the depths of my soul and I commit to following You fully and wholeheartedly. I surrender my will that I may come and see You through faith and not my own limited sight. Amen.

THIS WAS MY LAST WEAK!

"Finally, be strong in the Lord
and in the strength of his might."
(Ephesians 6:10)

*"Only he who can say, 'The Lord is the strength of my life'
can go on to say, 'Of whom shall I be afraid?'"*
— Alexander MacLaren[12]

Day 9

THE TABLE TALK

Many times in life we make declarations about what will take place in our future. We tweak old failures by using different approaches, and we change the names of old ways, all in an effort to say we have achieved our resolutions. We must realize our tomorrow will not be any different than our today if our hearts are still in the same place as they were yesterday. It's so easy to get caught up in the idea of celebrating change, but have we really changed our habits or has time just passed us by?

In order for us to experience true change, we have to understand the authority and power Christ Jesus has given us (Ephesians 1:19). We must use that authority wisely and realize that as we move forward from day to day, year to year, some things in our lives must be remembered, some things retained, and some things released. God's purpose must be our priority.

What we allow in our lives is what we become, and what we receive is what we perceive. Our job is to suit up for the days ahead, to stand strong in our Lord and in the power of His might. We must refuse to hold on to our old habits, because we are new in Christ Jesus. We will no longer compromise and give in to our fears. Our oppositions will shrink based on the strength of our faith in the Lord! Paul in his epistle to the Ephesians urges Christians to put on the armor of the Lord: the belt of truth and the breastplate of righteousness. By walking as one clad in the armor of God's strength, we can defeat temptation and make choices consistent with faith in the Lord.

Our oppositions will shrink based on the strength of our faith in the Lord!

John Flavel said, "The carnal person fears man not God. The strong Christian fears God, not man. The weak Christian fears man too much and God too little."[13] Which Christian are we? As children of God we belong to the spiritual realm as well as the natural realm. This means we have spiritual foes who can use the natural realm to create battles in our lives. This is the reason we need not just the physical strength but also the spiritual strength to face our battles. The spiritual realm, of course, supersedes the natural realm, so we should know how to walk in the spirit in order to impact the natural.

The carnal mind, which operates by the five senses and not by the Spirit of God, conflicts with God without authority or power. Only one person has absolute authority—Christ Jesus. "And they were all amazed and said to one another, 'What is this word? For with authority and power he commands the unclean spirits, and they come out!'" (Luke 4:36). In Luke 9:1, Jesus gave His disciples power and authority "over all demons and to cure diseases." We too possess authority based on our position in Christ; our union with Him gives us absolute authority. Because of our authority, the enemy tries to get us to compromise this power by attempting to insert fear, unbelief, rebellion, tainted thoughts, and emotions.

Our enemy knows our weaknesses and will seek to exploit them. Even at our best, we are weak and need God's strength. Being included in God's kingdom-work means the enemy will try to stop us. We must not shrink back from these attacks nor seek them out, but we must stand firmly in the power of His might. Paul admonished Timothy to endure hardness as a good soldier and not get entangled with the affairs of this life. This message is for us as well. Let us turn back to our source of strength, Christ Jesus, in order to withstand the shock of the battle. No human power alone can stop the devil's schemes. Only God Himself holds the power to fight and win.

God can and has already "disarmed the rulers and authorities and put them to open shame, by triumphing over them in him" (Colossians 2:15). The very same power that raised Jesus from the dead lives in believers by the Holy Spirit and empowers us to win our spiritual battles. We have only to remember the victory won on the cross by our Savior, Jesus Christ, and know that this power allows us to declare, "This was my last weak!"

A SHEEP'S REQUEST

Heavenly Father, may I always look to You for my source of strength. Grant me wisdom to change those habits in my life that separate me from You. Help me to seek You in all things, standing in truth and righteousness in the power of Your might. Amen.

DON'T TAKE IN WHAT GOD SAID KEEP OUT

"When Israel grew strong, they put the Canaanites to forced labor, but did not drive them out completely" (v. 28).
(Judges 1:28–33)

"No man doth safely rule but he that hath learned gladly to obey."
— Thomas á Kempis[14]

Day 10

THE TABLE TALK

There is a great gulf between what "once was" and what "now is." We are new creatures in Christ; old things have passed away and all things have become new. If we fail to embrace this understanding as God intended for us to, we will become frustrated in our journey. Since the enemy is not able to frustrate the Hand of the Sender, he tries his best to agitate the receivers (us). When we compromise, mix up, or contaminate our "once was" with our "now is," we can undermine the purpose God has for us. As in our passage today, the Lord commands us to kill and drive out certain beliefs and thoughts so that the enemy cannot use them to agitate or humiliate us.

Too often, instead of obeying God and destroying things in our lives as he commanded, our pride has us twisted up and participating with the problem, believing it is the solution. Where pride grows, grace withers. Disobedience stirred with obedience is still simply disobedience. Even in our refusal to obey God it may feel as if we have gained ground, but there is no true reaping—no true victory because we become comfortable with the compromise. The Bible makes it clear that God expects strict adherence to His commands. The more we are willing to compromise, the more we find ourselves being hindered and giving into the enemy.

The Israelites were told by God to completely destroy the Canaanites and other nations because He had prepared this ground for their inheritance. The Lord did not want them to become influenced against Him, which is ultimately what happened. Israel did not heed the voice of the Lord. Although they gained, they were not victorious because they became comfortable with the concession they made to not destroy the people, but to keep them as slaves for hard labor.

When we choose not to destroy what God has commanded us to remove from our lives, we become overburdened.

How often have we refused to reject those things which the Lord has specifically spoken to us about? Our choice opens a foothold to the enemy. He is prepared to do anything to anybody as long as he can get somebody to do something. If the enemy can keep us humiliated with our sins, we will never be able to praise the Lord for how they were covered. When we choose not to destroy what God has commanded us to remove from our lives, we become overburdened. We deplete the strategies God gave us for wiping out the enemy's schemes, and then guilt begins to settle in our hearts. Satan wants us to believe that because of our disobedience we will never be anything, do anything, or be worthy to approach the Lord. The key is that we are not approaching the Lord based on our worthiness but on Jesus's worthiness. The enemy's accusations will always drive us away from the cross, but the Holy Spirit will always bring us back to the cross and resurrection.

A SHEEP'S REQUEST

Heavenly Father, I thank You that I no longer have to live under the guilt of "once was" because in You my "now is" is greater. Teach me to obey and destroy those things in my life that allow the enemy to agitate and humiliate me. Thank You for covering what I have committed to You and for removing the feelings of guilt from my heart and mind. Thank You for my newness in You, my "now is!" Amen.

BY HIS HANDS

"Know that the Lord, he is God!
It is he who made us, and we are his;
we are his people, and the sheep of his pasture." (v. 3)
(Psalm 100:1–5)

*"We're not being reared by the shepherd to be sold for slaughter,
but his sheep will live forever."*
— Toby Powers[15]

Day 11

THE TABLE TALK

Psalm 100 is one of the most known and well-loved psalms in the Bible. It is a humbling privilege to realize that we are His sheep and that He is our loving, caring shepherd. He will not sell us to be slaughtered as earthly shepherds will do. God delights in us and sent His Son, Jesus, to die for our sins. If we have accepted Him as our Savior, we will live with Him forever.

God has created us and is our shepherd—the one responsible for our well-being and enlightenment. We must recognize the origin of our being and adore our maker because we are not self-made. He made us all from nothing in His image, and without the help or accompaniment of anyone else. We can take no credit for existing, for we are the sole right and property of God. His Lordship is not something we accomplished; it is something we recognize and submit to. We cannot have what the shepherd produces without having the shepherd as Lord of our lives. As His sheep, we are called to serve and obey Him while expressing heartfelt gratefulness.

God knows His sheep by name and leads them. They know His voice and they follow Him. We must assume the mantle of being God's faithful flock. We must thank and praise Him for all our blessings, both in this world and the world to come. We must not doubt Him, for the Good Shepherd does not abandon His sheep. Matthew 18:12–13 tells us that if Jesus has 100 sheep and 99 are safely in His fold, He will go look for the missing one. What a blessing to know that all of us are so valuable to Him and never beyond His loving care. There is nothing we can do to make Him love us more—or less.

God has taken us as both His joy and His burden by giving us free will, which enables us to stray from His flock. He knows that left to our own devices we will go astray. No longer does God expect tribute in the sense of ritual sacrifice, but He longs for love and obedience from His sheep. Keeping His commandments, gathering together for prayer, spreading the gospel, trusting in Him—these are the sacrifices we as God's sheep can offer Him. We are His people, the sheep of His pastures, and we enter His gates with praise and thanksgiving. That is the proper way for us to approach God, with hearts filled with thanksgiving. Gratitude is an attitude, not something we just say or do. A sacrifice of praise always costs us something. We must release our pride and the weight of sin that keeps us from giving Him the praise He deserves.

There are many trials along the way, to be sure, challenging our faith and commitment to God, our creator and redeemer. If we follow the righteous path set before us by the Shepherd, we will be triumphant. God's care is unconditional, but He asks us to be faithful sheep who listen to and obey His words. Through prayer, faith, gratefulness, and servitude toward God and others, we can please the Lord and will be placed at His table in the afterlife. Let us be the sheep who follow the Shepherd every day, overcoming all obstacles with His love and guidance.

A SHEEP'S REQUEST

Heavenly Father, You made us in Your image. You gave us dominion over creatures of the land and sea. Yet we are weak and require Your protection and care. We are Your sheep, and You are our Shepherd. We offer You our humble praise and thanksgiving.

Still we may stray. Help us follow You along the path of righteousness in our thoughts, words, and deeds every day, so that we may join You in Your eternal kingdom forever. Amen.

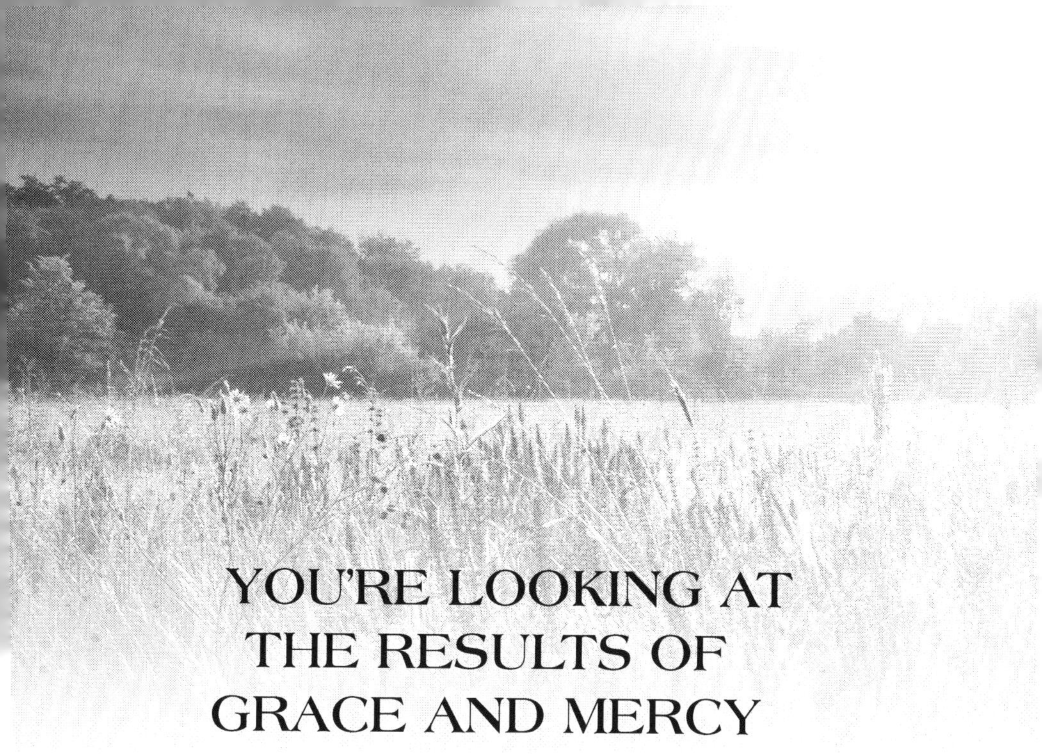

YOU'RE LOOKING AT THE RESULTS OF GRACE AND MERCY

"The saying is trustworthy and deserving of full acceptance, that Christ Jesus came into the world to save sinners, of whom I am the foremost. But I received mercy for this reason, that in me, as the foremost, Jesus Christ might display his perfect patience as an example to those who were to believe in him for eternal life."
(1 Timothy 1:15-16)

"Reader! if you would know the heart of your sin—then you must know the sins of your heart! . . . Until we *taste* the *bitterness of our own misery*—we shall never *relish* the *sweetness of God's mercy*. Until we see how *foul* our sins have made us—we shall never pay our tribute of praise to Christ for *washing* us."
— William Secker[16]

Day 12

THE TABLE TALK

What creates the loud voice that shouts victory or the cry like no other or the unique praise to the Lord? Such comes from our testimony. You can tell if one's testimony is truly birthed from memory or something that has been rehearsed simply by observing how it first impacts the one who is testifying. It would be impossible for listeners to get more excited about a testimony than the person giving it because it does not belong to us. The core of our personal testimony does not only come from the fact that we have been saved. It comes from a deeper understanding of by whom, from whom, out of where, and from what we were saved! Once we fully comprehend what has been done for us, then and only then, can we begin to take hold of the grace and mercy that has been extended to us by our Father. In His abundant mercy, He does not treat us as our sins deserve. Because of His never-failing grace, we receive what we do not deserve—unearned favor!

He did not choose us because we were worthy, but the act of choosing us makes us worthy.

At times we seem to take for granted and forget just how much cleaning up the Lord had to do with us, which explains why our praise, worship, and obedience are often not at the level they should be. Our gratitude should increase consistently for we all deserve death, but because our Lord and Savior is both gracious and merciful, He extended kindness toward us and delivered us from judgment. God does not owe us anything, and we deserve nothing from Him. We should recall frequently that a holy God rescued us from sin, washed us in the blood of the Lamb, and now calls us His sons and daughters. What a supreme expression of His great love for us!

God daily bestows upon us unmerited grace and mercy. He has shown both compassion and generosity toward us beyond our ability to even imagine. While we were yet in our sinful state, He granted us the gift of salvation through His abundant love. God's purpose is designed to include those with a paralyzed past, because His mercy goes beyond it. He did not choose us because we were worthy, but the act of choosing us makes us worthy.

A SHEEP'S REQUEST

Heavenly Father, thank You for not punishing me as my sins deserve. You have blessed me in spite of the fact that I do not deserve it. I am so unworthy, yet You extend kindness continually and redeemed my life. Every day I live is an act of Your mercy and a result of Your grace. I am eternally grateful for Your love, blessing, and favor. Amen.

A PURPOSE IN MY PAIN

"But he said to me, 'My grace is sufficient for you,
for my power is made perfect in weakness.'
Therefore I will boast all the more gladly of my weaknesses,
so that the power of Christ may rest upon me."
(2 Corinthians 12:9)

"The Lord gets His best soldiers out of the highlands of affliction."
— Charles Spurgeon[17]

Day 13

THE TABLE TALK

Saints, all over the world at the beginning of each new year we will witness multitudes of individuals declaring what is going to take place ahead for them. We place timelines on certain successes (New Year's resolutions). We set out to make the upcoming year a new and better year than years past. Statistics show that only 8 percent of people achieve their resolutions. In reality if our heart doesn't change, our tomorrow will not be any different than our yesterday. We will constantly be on the hamster wheel of life, going nowhere fast. Therefore, our desire to seek change for our lives should be spiritually, not naturally motivated.

The work of Christ in our lives gives us strength, power, and authority to change. We have been given dominion over the enemy and are equipped with the tools we need to make changes spiritually, which will in turn affect our lives naturally. Although we may want to change in principle we often refuse to change our habits.

God's purpose must be our priority.

We can't take everything with us from this year into the next. God's purpose must be our priority, for what we allow in our lives is what we will become. If our worry list is long, then we are viewing God as smaller than our worries. If our fears are greater than our faith, we will become hopeless and despair will grip our heart. We must not operate in our own strength, but in the power of God's might. Then and only then will we see His power made perfect in our weakness. We will see a purpose in our pain. We do not possess strength equal to that of the Lord, so at our weakest times we can see that His power is the greatest. God has an infinite variety of options for using His strength. Unlike us who enjoy boasting in or showing off our strength, God operates in power, strength, and sufficiency every time He does anything. God is omni-sufficient. Only His grace is able to sustain us.

When we are weak, it forces us to trust in God alone. We become less self-dependent and wholly God-dependent. Why throughout the Bible did God allow things to go so terrifyingly wrong before He rescued His people (Daniel in the lion's den; Isaac got all the way to the altar; the three Hebrew boys in the fiery furnace)? God wanted them to realize that He alone was their help and His sufficient grace would see them through any trial. God desires the same for us, calling us to rest in Him, trust Him with all our heart, and lean not to our own understanding, so that we may be anxious for nothing as we trust in His sufficiency. God wants it to be abundantly clear that He alone will intervene and rescue us from our painful situations.

No one goes about life seeking trials and suffering. In fact, we would rather avoid them altogether. Nonetheless, suffering plays a role in our life as a Christian. Our suffering, whether physical pain, financial struggles, or loss of a loved one, is not random or arbitrary. God uses these trials to make us more like Christ and grow our faith in Him. We are weak so that His strength can provide us with deliverance. Sin has made us imperfect, so it is through Jesus Christ that we can willingly embrace Him in faith and gain our strength. Today we declare to ourselves that we will be strong in the Lord! Whatever pain I am enduring, no hurt is wasted in the life of a child of God.

A SHEEP'S REQUEST

Heavenly Father, thank You for the power and authority You have given me over the enemy. I confess, Lord, that sometimes I am weak, lose sight spiritually and compromise my faith. I pray now for increased strength that I may operate in the absolute power that You have made available to me through Christ Jesus. I am equipped and suited up for the days ahead to make changes and stand strong in the Lord. Amen.

FULL OF ACTIVITY BUT BEARING NO FRUIT

"On the following day, when they came from Bethany,
he was hungry. And seeing in the distance a fig tree in leaf,
he went to see if he could find anything on it.
When he came to it, he found nothing but leaves,
for it was not the season for figs" (vv. 12–13).
(Mark 11:12–14)

"The heart is the mainspring."
— Smith Wigglesworth[18]

Day 14

THE TABLE TALK

This act by Jesus may puzzle those of us not familiar with fig trees in the Middle East and their fruit-bearing cycles. At the time that Jesus approached the tree, it should have had some fruit on it, either first fruits or possibly some of its main crop. The fact that leaves were showing without fruit indicated the tree was barren, and Jesus merely cut it down with faith rather than an axe, since it could not serve a viable purpose.

This resembles the modern phenomenon of misleading claims or false advertisement that we have all experienced at some point or another in life. A particular item or product we desire is presented as one thing (a useful fig tree) yet upon closer inspection is not at all what we expected. In today's passage, Jesus cursed a fig tree to point out that its impressive exterior (bearing leaves) was deceptive in that it bore no fruit. The tree displayed a show of life, but as one writer stated, it offered "promise without performance."

This is an important lesson for us to consider when looking at our own lives. Do our exterior appearances show something different than what we are really producing? We must carefully examine our hearts so that we don't confuse the leaves with the fruit. In order for us to fulfill the purpose God has for our lives, we must bear fruit. He knows what He has planted in us, and we must yield to His pruning or suffer a loss of fruit. Although the pruning process is not enjoyable, we must learn to embrace it, for this is when the Father refines our character by cutting out the greed, pride, bitterness, and other sin in our lives.

Vinedressers aggressively prune their vines to avoid disease and rot. In the winter when you walk through a vineyard, it looks like a wasteland, but it is not what it seems. A season of pruning must pass in order for the fruit and harvest to come. Pruning spares the nourishment of the vine for the branches that are most viable. God prunes us so that we will bear more fruit. He is making it possible for us to live a life that will have a greater impact for His glory. Let us not resist the difficult but necessary work that He desires to do in us.

We must carefully examine our hearts so that we don't confuse the leaves with the fruit.

To bear good fruit requires work, time, patience, and perseverance. If no fruit is growing on our branches, maybe we have lost connection to the vine. Maybe we are spiritually dead or dying, which means we will be cut off. To avoid facing God's spiritual shears, we must allow Him to prepare us for a new harvest. God knows how to tend to us. Maybe He was not pleased with the last harvest, so through His great love He has begun to work on us for next year. He is not content to leave us where we are but longs to hear us agree to His pruning so that He can accomplish His work through us. God wants us not only to bear fruit but also to bear an abundance of fruit to glorify Him, not just use up the ground. For us, bearing fruit is always in season, because professing without producing is simply not an option. Jesus Himself mentioned the empty acts of worship by the Pharisees and Sadducees—impressive in appearance but hollow in faith.

Symbolically, the fig tree also represented the spiritual deadness of Israel, which was very religious outwardly but spiritually barren. As Spirit-led people our lives should be full of activity and flourishing in the production of fruit (love, peace, joy, longsuffering, kindness, goodness, faithfulness, gentleness, and self-control), not just give an appearance of religiosity. Most importantly, God judges fruitlessness and expects us as His children to bear fruit. If we are going to grow we have to realize that we will certainly have times of pruning. We must have the sinful parts of our lives cut back, so that a new season of harvest can come and that all we do will be for God's glory!

A SHEEP'S REQUEST

Heavenly Father, let me deliver what I am displaying. I yield to Your pruning so that I may fulfill the purpose You have designed for my life. Let my life continue to display the fruit that You instilled in me and not fruit of my own flesh. Amen.

ESCAPING STRIFE'S TRAPS

"For they vex you with their wiles, wherewith they have beguiled you in the matter of Peor, and in the matter of Cozbi, the daughter of a prince of Midian, their sister, which was slain in the day of the plague for Peor's sake" (25:18 KJV).
(Numbers 22:1–6; 25:16–18)

"Outside of the will of God, there is nothing I want.
And in the will of God there is nothing I fear."
— A.W. Tozer[19]

Day 15

THE TABLE TALK

Remember this absolutely essential truth: the Lord has already proven Himself to be amazingly good and perfectly upright in His dealings with all humanity. Whatever God says goes and everything He does is in line with His perfect will. He has already seen every adverse circumstance we will encounter and has made a way for us to escape in advance. Although sometimes we look for God to do things the way we think is best, He will not create a new way because He has already provided the best way. We must keep in mind that He is not the answerer nor the responder to the challenges we face in life; He is the initiator of those challenges. He knew what trials and difficulties would come our way before we were ever born, which is why He tells us to cast our cares upon Him.

When we find ourselves looking for a different way than what God has already provided, we are walking in disobedience.

This is why we should seek God first when problems arise. He already knows the solution and wants to show us the way. When we find ourselves looking for a different way than what God has already provided, we are walking in disobedience.

Too often we trust ourselves to figure out solutions to our problems, allowing the enemy to attack and cause strife. When strife comes on the scene, it opposes who we are in Christ and places us in conflict with God. Strife usually comes just before a major harvest, and if we allow it to remain it will destroy our produce, annihilate relationships, cause pain, place our life on hold, and quench the Holy Spirit. Israel was on their way to experiencing the fulfillment of a promise from God when strife reared its ugly head by way of the Midianites (their name means "strife"). This is why God commanded Israel to destroy them. He knew the Midianites had and would continue to cause strife. We must be able to discern when the enemy is trying to stir up strife in our lives, so that we can seek God for a way of escape according to His plan.

We must not be afraid to confront evil, as God has commanded the children of Israel time and again. Some evil must be destroyed, but Jesus has given us another way to meet other evils (as well as non-believers)—the message of faith (Matt 28:16–20). By spreading the Word of God we can decrease evil and increase harmony throughout the world.

A SHEEP'S REQUEST

Heavenly Father, help me to escape strife's traps. Teach me to cast my cares on You and accept that Your plan is what is best for me. Grant me wisdom and discernment to recognize when the enemy is attempting to lure me into strife and contention, so that I do not lose focus on Your plan for my life. Give me the strength to resist the prideful seeking of another way when You have already provided the best path for my life. I yield to Your leading and Your will for me and will resist heresy while spreading Your truth. Amen.

WAIT

"But they who wait for the Lord shall renew their strength;
they shall mount up with wings like eagles;
they shall run and not be weary;
they shall walk and not faint" (v. 31).
(Isaiah 40:27–31)

"Those who do not hope cannot wait;
but if we hope for that we see not,
then do we with patience wait for it."
— Charles Spurgeon[20]

Day 16

THE TABLE TALK

Sometimes God's prolonged patience feels as if it is delaying the results we expect to see. We fail to understand why we wait, with our prayers seemingly ignored. This can lead to doubt; we may question God's abilities and love for us. Because He does not act as we think He should *when* we think He should, we conclude He cannot act as we think He would (or even that He has forsaken us).

We fail to comprehend that God never has emergencies. He is not moved or rushed by things we think are critical. His action or inaction is not based upon what we deem to be pressing situations. He knows our plight and may choose to give us time to work on it ourselves or grow strong in faith. Isaiah 40:27–31 focuses on strength and that we are renewed in strength implies times of weakness. We must remember that God's strength is made perfect in our weakness. We cannot allow the exaggerated urgency of our "right now" moments to pressure us into moving ahead of God and ultimately making a costly mistake. God does not work on our time nor does He exert His almighty power for us at the first moment we implore Him to come to our aid.

We cannot allow the exaggerated urgency of our "right now" moments to pressure us into moving ahead of God and ultimately making a costly mistake.

We are to wait on the Lord with hope and confident expectancy. When we do so we demonstrate our trust in Him. He does not make us wait just for the sake of waiting or to see how long we can hold out. Sometimes we wonder why God appears to delay in answering us, but we must be assured that He will come through at the perfect time. To wait properly requires us to totally depend on Him, allowing Him to work out His plan for our lives on His terms. This can be one of the most difficult things to do because by nature we are impatient and want quick results. We must learn to be still and rest in the Lord, knowing He is in complete control and will be faithful according to His promises. We have to relinquish our agenda and surrender our will in exchange for respite in Him. The Lord will never leave us or forsake us; waiting allows us to interchange our burdens for His power, purpose, and care. God wants us to leave the details of our lives with Him, and as long as we are involved He will not act on our behalf. The Lord simply wants us to do the work He has given us to do and fill our time with service to Him.

There is wisdom in the waiting and those who wait on the Lord will not be disappointed. Waiting on the Lord renews our strength (v. 31). Therefore, regardless of the trials and challenges we face, we have the blessed assurance God will strengthen us and come to our defense. We can be certain the Lord has what is best for us in mind. We can be confident of a positive outcome according to His will. We should not be dismayed when He delays His response but must wait on Him with a heart of patience, rooted and grounded in faith. The lessons we learn while waiting are the tools we will need when we finally get what we have been waiting for.

We must learn to seek God while waiting, for in those times we stand in a prime position to see His hand. Sometimes we can't believe God is going to come through, based on the logic of the situation as we understand it, but Isaiah gives us the solution—to wait on the Lord. When we refuse to exercise the discipline of waiting, we miss all the godly lessons between the asking and the getting. Isaiah reminds us that those who wait on the Lord will have renewed strength. Let us not lose heart while waiting, but determine today that we will learn to wait on the Lord that we might see His strength made perfect in our weakness.

A SHEEP'S REQUEST

Heavenly Father, help me to learn to wait on You. Sometimes I become discouraged and weary in my waiting, but I know You know best and will strengthen me. I pray my faith does not falter as I wait but that I will learn to seek You more during the process. Give me patience so that I may wait well and see Your hand at work in my life. Amen.

THE DANGER OF ALMOST

"But Saul and the people spared Agag and the best of the sheep and of the oxen and of the fattened calves and the lambs, and all that was good, and would not utterly destroy them. All that was despised and worthless they devoted to destruction" (v. 9).
(1 Samuel 15:1–11)

"Wherever you are, be all there.
Live to the hilt every situation
you believe to be the will of God."
— Jim Elliot[21]

Day 17

THE TABLE TALK

God knows in foresight what we can only see in hindsight. One would think the lessons learned from our previous experiences would be enough evidence to show us that God knows exactly what He is doing. We should have gained enough strength from Him bringing us through our past obstacles to willingly follow His next directions. We should be able to tell our problems, no matter how big, that our God is bigger and that we know He can do it, whatever it is! But often this is not the case. When pressures or challenges consume us, we look within ourselves or seek counsel from other friends.

God wants us to wholly depend on Him and trust Him without reservation. Trust isn't necessarily an easy thing to do, but it is required in order for us to have a relationship with God. So why is trusting God so difficult for us to do? What causes us to look to others for solutions to our problems? Disobedience is one of the primary things that keep us from trusting God. He has given us free will and with it comes the option to obey or not to obey. Obedience is a choice and requires standing against a powerful desire to disobey. A thin, unseen line has God's patience on one side and His wrath the other. Once we have made the decision to walk on the wrong side of the line, we now have to be invited back into fellowship with God through His grace and mercy.

This is why we must quickly identify disobedience in our lives, because if left unchecked, it becomes easier and easier to cross the line and refuse to submit to God's authority. This is when our will becomes stronger than God's will, and we begin to make His voice sound like our voice.

There is no middle ground and no peace in living a lukewarm life.

Continued disobedience leads to rebellion in that we renounce and refuse to come under God's authority. There is no middle ground and no peace in living a lukewarm life. We cannot serve two masters so we either pledge exclusive allegiance to Christ or to the enemy.

In our scripture passage today we see the lawless state of the children of Israel. God told them specifically to wipe out the Amalekites, but they disobeyed just as we do at times. We do not realize the reason the Lord desires that we obey Him and leave some things behind is He knows those things will eventually bring us down. Most of the hardships we go through are a result of ignoring God's warnings to us. When God tells us to kill the sin, He means kill the sin. He knows one sin easily leads to more and greater sin. That leaves an open door for Satan to try to convince us to take hold of those things that will continue to hinder us and bring divine chastisement upon us. The enemy wants to see us fall prey to the consequences of our disobedience. God gave Satan a legal right to darkness, which is why he tries to take us out of the light.

God has promises appended to everything He commands. Saul thought he was using good judgment by not killing Agag, the Amalekite king, and his good resources. Like us, Saul did not have the foresight of the Lord. It is not hard to conceive of King Agag regaining his power, using those resources, and later destroying Saul. Saul placed his judgment ahead of the Lord God's and paid for it by losing the kingdom.

If we do His will, favor and blessings will follow. If we disobey, certain other promises will follow our disobedience. We must know what God said to do and not to do. Partial disobedience is simply disobedience. Either we will choose to trust and obey God or we will not, but almost trusting and obeying Him is not an option.

A SHEEP'S REQUEST

Heavenly Father, I pray that I will be fully devoted to You. Lord, help me to trust You completely and surrender my will to Your will, even when I do not understand at the time. I desire to obey Your commands and live for You only! Amen.

WHEN THE ENEMY COMES

"Put on the whole armor of God, that you may be able to stand against the schemes of the devil" (v. 11).
(Ephesians 6:10–18)

"The joy of the Lord will arm us against the assaults of our spiritual enemies, and put our mouths out of taste for those pleasures with which the tempter baits his hooks."
— Matthew Henry[22]

Day 18

THE TABLE TALK

All of us have some things in life we would like to restart or do over. Often times we struggle with unhealthy habits we desire to stop, yet despite our best intentions to change, we continue in our ways. We have done many things we know we should not have done, things we brought with us from year to year that God told us to leave behind, and things He told us to bring that we do not have. In our disobedience we find ourselves stuck in a vicious cycle, yearning for a fresh start but never following through.

Our ability to make real and lasting changes to our life is limited, even when we try our hardest. If we rely solely on our own positive thinking or our indomitable resolve to change our ways, we will not get very far. The Father loves His children too much to let us remain stuck on a hamster wheel, going nowhere fast. He wants to help us become our best selves and experience the best life possible in Him, but we must cooperate with His work in our lives. This work often comes in the form of challenging seasons and attacks from the enemy.

Do you realize how valuable you are to God? Our high value provokes spiritual battles. The moment we surrendered our lives to the Lord, the enemy geared up for battle against us because he too knows our worth. The mere fact we are under attack by the enemy is proof positive we are headed in the right direction. The enemy is always at war against us because of our birthright. He opposes any advancement and tries to intercept breakthroughs in our life. The attacks will first come to the weak or neglected areas of our lives, so that God can reveal to us what needs to be strengthened. The smallest details have profound significance because Satan is an opportunist always looking to find our frailties and how we are not following the strategic ways of the Holy Spirit. God has already given us the power and spiritual weapons needed to defeat him, leaving us without reason to fear.

It is impossible for us to embrace greatness and new heights in the Lord with small-mindedness, doubt, and fear.

God longs to strengthen our hands for these battles, but we repeatedly cling to the very things that weaken us. If we don't surrender our vulnerable areas to God, we will continue to struggle and won't see Him fighting our battles. Too often we attempt to carry more than we have to or engage in battles that God did not ordain, leaving us wearied and burdened. At times we should pause to assess whether our actions and words are aligned with God or the enemy. Are we speaking defeat or victory? It is impossible for us to embrace greatness and new heights in the Lord with small-mindedness, doubt, and fear.

Some may think it strange, but we as Christians recognize that spiritual warfare is real. There will always be battles on our journey with the Lord. How we fight and the weapons we choose will determine whether we win or lose. "For the weapons of our warfare are not of the flesh but have divine power to destroy strongholds" (2 Corinthians 10:4). Victorious Christians win first and then go to war simply to collect. A defeated Christian goes to war first and then seeks to win.

A SHEEP'S REQUEST

Heavenly Father, thank You for showing me my value and that the battles only come to make me stronger. I pray that in those times, I speak words of wisdom, life, and victory. Help me daily to put on Your whole armor that I may be equipped to stand against the enemy's fiery darts. Lord, I surrender my weakness to You so that I may have strength to fight my battles with courage, using godly wisdom. In You, I am more than a conqueror and have victory over every battle that comes my way! Amen.

FROM FIRE TO FUNCTION

"If I say, 'I will not mention him,
or speak any more in his name,'
there is in my heart as it were a burning fire
shut up in my bones, and I am weary with holding it in,
and I cannot" (v. 9).
(Jeremiah 20:7–13)

"The difference between perseverance and obstinacy is that one comes from a strong will, and the other from a strong won't."
— Henry Ward Beecher[23]

Day 19

THE TABLE TALK

It is easy to feel at a disadvantage when we do not fully understanding God's goodness. Without such an understanding we can allow ourselves to believe that He is only lifting us up to tear us down again. Thus, we must take confidence in this truth—God is immutable. His goodness can never change in any way. He will never be better than He is now, nor will He ever be any less good. Everything He will ever do will always be good because God is good! His love for us flows out of His goodness. He deals bountifully, tenderly, and kindly with us. His mercy flows freely toward us and His grace is applied to our lives.

One would think if we knew all of this about God, we would never challenge His will for us, but no: sometimes the misfortunes of life cause us to want to throw in the towel. Sometimes we find ourselves locked in the traffic of being mocked, laughed at, or ridiculed (just like Jeremiah) for sharing good news in desperate situations.

God uses our experiences to fan the flame of our passion for Him.

Opposition has a way of proving our passion but not stopping it. We find in our scripture passage today that Jeremiah was denounced for announcing the seemingly impossible. He decided to resign from preaching God's will but immediately declared he could not resign. He tried to quit, but he could not quit, because God's truth was a part of his essence. He found God's Word to be like a fire shut up in his bones! This prophet is a perfect example of how God uses our experiences to fan the flame of our passion for Him.

Satan attempts to hinder our fire in three ways:

1. drown it with discouragement,
2. smother it with sorrow,
3. choke it out with controversy.

Nonetheless, we must say to ourselves that no matter how Satan tries to put out the fire God has placed inside us, we will not let the flame go out. We must tell of His goodness because keeping our testimony to ourselves will create heartburn. Faith is not always easy in the face of disappointment, yet we must, like Jeremiah, come to a place where our fire overrides our desires. God's fire will burn up our inherent (old) nature and warm up the new nature of faith.

The trials will come because we lack the ability explain to others what we have not yet experienced. How can we have an authentic testimony about God's goodness if we have not undergone trials and adversity? He places before us trials commensurate with our needs but not too formidable as to put out our flame. We can endure because it is the fire that makes us function.

Challenging situations can take us to the point of resignation that will only brings us back into consecration to hear the revelation about our obligation for our celebration! Evil will afflict the good. Nonetheless, we have free will and must choose God, for His wisdom outshines our doubts; in Him we will find everlasting salvation in heaven, if not here on earth. Cast aside doubts and spread faith in the Lord.

A SHEEP'S REQUEST

Heavenly Father, thank You for the various trials that serve to flame the fire in my life. Your goodness, mercy, and grace are unfathomable, and I cannot keep my testimony to myself. Use me to encourage others and tell of Your goodness, which will diminish evil in the world. I realize now it is the fire that makes me function, so I pray You will give me strength to stand when Satan tries to put out my flame. Amen.

STANDING ON THE PROMISES, NOT THE PREMISES

"But we have this treasure in earthen vessels,
that the excellency of the power may be of God,
and not of us" (v. 7).
(2 Corinthians 4:1–10)

"The permanence of God's character guarantees
the fulfillment of his promises."
— A.W Pink[24]

Day 20

THE TABLE TALK

We have testimonies non-believers witness but many times we are not aware of. Often, we are on display for a greater cause than what we can imagine. We don't know it until someone on the outside shares how our handling of a situation caused him or her to seek the Lord. We serve a covenant-keeping Savior and God uses us as an example of His promises. Although we are not exempt from the trials non-believers go through, we are exalted above the effect that they experience. Others are watching us to see how we handle our challenges and wonder where our strength comes from.

Our weakness is necessary because we must learn to grow and become wholly dependent on God. When we serve Him in weakness, He gets the glory. Then we become living testimonies of God's promises. Our trials are not to expose what we are made of, but instead demonstrate what God's power is like. Our role is to focus on the treasure within, not the vessel that holds it, so that God in turn will guard the vessel.

We must not confuse what we are going through with where we are going to.

So the Lord declares victory on all defeated ground to show the world that in us the end is just the beginning. This scripture bolsters us as Christians in the following ways. It reassures us that God will take care of us and others will see and be moved; however, it humbles us by reminding us that God and the sacrifice of

His Son, not we ourselves, give us our strength. J. Moltmann said, "In the promises [of God], the hidden future already announces itself and pushes its influence on the present through the hope it awakens."[25] We must not confuse what we are going through with where we are going to. In Christ, God overrules our circumstances and they become light afflictions compared to the greatness they are producing in us. He promises to see us through when we are troubled, perplexed, persecuted, and cast down. These are not signs of God's abandonment but signs of His activity in our lives. Look for God's fingerprints and we will see His promises at work. Remember, no trials, setbacks, or calamities have the power to destroy God's promises!

A SHEEP'S REQUEST

Heavenly Father, help me to recall and stand on your promises. May my life be an example to others of your power and your promises to see me through any challenge I face in life. I pray I learn more and more how to trust you. I am waiting expectantly for the greatness that will come as I learn to endure my trials, for I know they have a purpose and are filtered through Your great love for me. Amen.

WHAT TO EXPECT WHEN YOU ARE EXPECTING

"And when the south wind blew softly, supposing that they had obtained their purpose, loosing thence, they sailed close by Crete. But not long after there arose against it a tempestuous wind, called Euroclydon" (27:13–14 KJV).

(Acts 23:11 and 27:13–25)

"True faith is never found alone;
it is always accompanied by expectation."
— A.W. Tozer[26]

Day 21

THE TABLE TALK

Many times believers are discouraged because they do not understand what it means to expect. When something resists us while we wait, it can sap the strength of our faith. The battle does not start until we begin expecting. Whenever we expect something from God it triggers other expectations from the opposing side. We have the enemy's expectations as well as the flesh's expectations, and both try to fulfill theirs over the Lord's. We must, therefore, cover ourselves by putting on the whole armor of God so that we may be able to stand against the trickery of the enemy. If Satan sees us kneeling, he will realize we are standing—standing on God's promises.

Everything we do shows that we either expect God to do what He said in His Word or that we don't expect it to come to pass.

Doubt may arise because of others' evil actions or our own personal storms. Whether we are deterred by a situation or a storm at sea, we must remain steadfast. Paul was one of the most steadfast evangelists of the early Christian movement; yet, even he wondered if he would be able to journey to all the places he needed to go to spread the gospel. Paul should not have worried, for God was with him and took him where he was called. We are God's army spreading his Word. We should trust that God has a job for us and nothing will prevent us from finishing it— except our own fears. For this reason, we must command ourselves to remain anchored and trust God. Sometimes we allow ourselves to get troubled by the side effects, but the side effects are what let us know that we are "expecting." Everything we do shows we either expect God to do what He said in His Word or that we don't expect it to come to pass. Expectations based on human assumptions can cause doubt, but we can expect God to do exactly what He says He will do. His promises are absolutely sound. When we anticipate good things, we open the door to God's plans. God is looking for those who are eagerly waiting for Him, but we have to be expecting Him to move in our lives.

God expects us to hold fast to the confession of our expectation without wavering. Many struggle to believe God is good, especially when (what they perceive to be) bad things happen in their lives. We sometimes easily allow ourselves to believe that God withholds good things from us and is not concerned with what happens in our lives. God is aware when we experience pain, and He cares about every aspect of our lives, responding out of goodness and grace. He reigns and rules over all things, and nothing happens to us by accident. If we truly anticipate the blessings of God, we will have to condition ourselves. We must enter His presence with eagerness and expectancy. Sometimes we may arrive at our blessing by way of storm, and we may even lose some things along the way. Once we truly take inventory of our lives, we realize those things were not needed. God will never leave us comfortless, and it is in the waiting that we learn what He expects when we are expecting to receive from Him.

A SHEEP'S REQUEST

Heavenly Father, help me to not be troubled as I expectantly wait to receive from You. You know exactly what I am in need of, and I can expect You to provide because You promised to supply my needs. You also know the desires of my heart, and if I delight myself in You, You will grant them according to Your will. Amen.

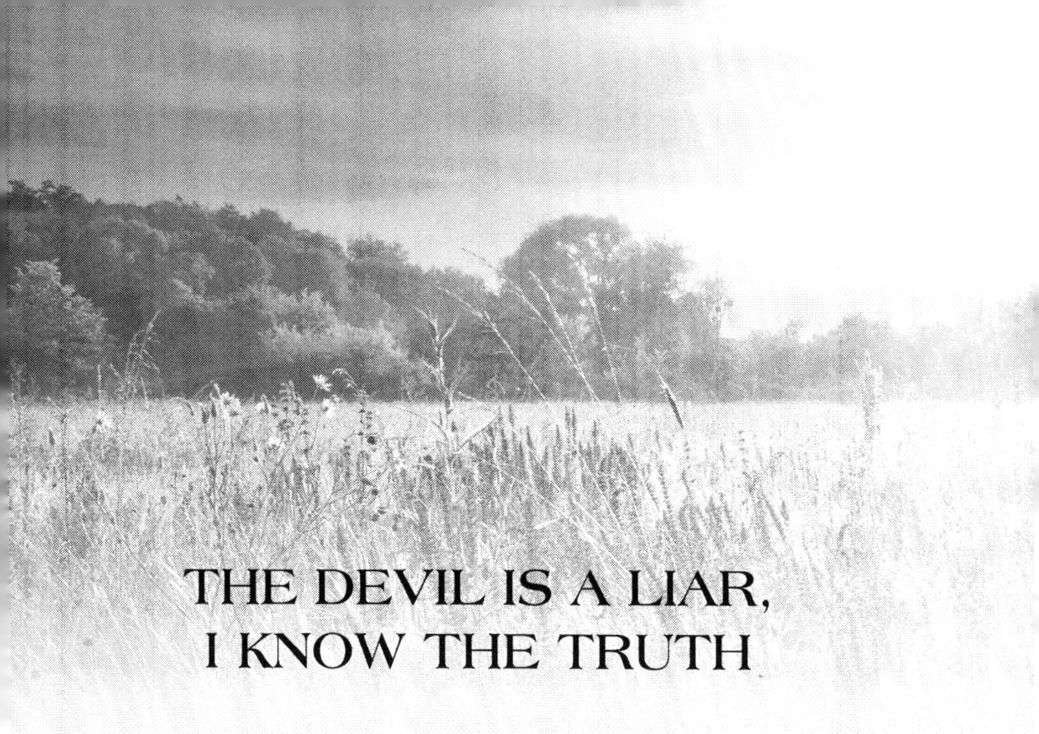

THE DEVIL IS A LIAR, I KNOW THE TRUTH

"As he was saying these things, many believed in him. So Jesus said to the Jews who had believed him, 'If you abide in my word, you are truly my disciples, and you will know the truth, and the truth will set you free.'"
(John 8:30–32)

"The gospel is not speculation but fact.
It is truth, because it is the record of a Person who is the Truth."
— Alexander MacLaren[27]

Day 22

THE TABLE TALK

Many believers will quickly accept a lie because they do not know the truth. Do you realize the enemy has engineered a take down before we even rise up to start our day? All believers have a bull's-eye on our backs; the enemy is targeting us in an effort to get us to surrender to his lies. He tries to get us to receive his lies and repeat them. We only say and do what we know. If the enemy is able to get us to believe his lies, we can become confused and unsure about what we think we know. If we don't walk in the truth, we will walk in a lie. Augustine said, "If you believe what you like in the gospel, and reject what you don't like, it's not the gospel you believe but yourself."[28] This is why it is critically important for us to know the truth—not our own truth, but the absolute, unadulterated truth of God's Word.

We must not be satisfied to just know about the truth, but we must desire to know the truth! Just because someone does not believe the truth does not render it false. Even if we mistakenly fail to accept God's Word as truth, we will still experience the consequences of it. The Father of Lies seeks to kill the truth. He tried to kill Jesus, and he desires to do the same to us. Falsehoods can only be stopped when met with disapproving ears. In order for us to keep from falling prey to the lies, we must continue walking in the truth. To continue means to "maintain a condition or course of action without interruption,"[29] which is paramount to our existence. Otherwise, we will begin to walk out the lies, and instead of moving forward in our journey with the Lord, we will actually be moving backwards.

We must tell ourselves that we will not entertain or give any credence to the lies of the enemy.

Knowing the truth causes us to fight from victory instead of fighting for victory because the truth is that Christ has already won. Satan's power is in the lies he wants us to accept. If we renounce the liar, his lies have no power over us. Knowing the truth causes our character to become stronger than our circumstances because there are no circumstances greater than the truth that we know. We must tell ourselves we will not entertain or give any credence to the lies of the enemy. Because we know the truth, Jesus, and because He lives in us, we don't have to believe anything the enemy says. Our God's promises are true and He will fulfill His word in our lives just as Jesus taught us!

A SHEEP'S REQUEST

Heavenly Father, help me to know and hide the truth in my heart so that I am not deceived by the Father of Lies. I desire to continue walking in the truth daily, so that I may recognize and combat the enemy's lies. Thank You, Lord, for setting me free by the truth of Your Word! Amen.

DIG WHEREVER YOU ARE ASKED TO DWELL

"And he moved from there and dug another well,
and they did not quarrel over it. So he called its name
Rehoboth, saying, 'For now the Lord has made room for us,
and we shall be fruitful in the land'" (v. 22).
(Genesis 26:17–25)

"Obedience is the only reality.
It is faith visible, faith acting,
and faith manifest."
— *J.C. Ryle*[30]

Day 23

THE TABLE TALK

Have you ever noticed whenever God gives a promise He will often try our faith? As I was sitting on my patio this week, I noticed the wind blowing hard against the trees causing them to sway back and forth as if they would break. As the trees swayed I could hear a stretching sound as if the roots were contending with the wind and taking a firmer hold on the ground. Our faith needs to take a firm hold when we are faced with various adverse situations. What shakes, twists, or upsets our rest in God's provision comes from trying to understand His motives and not His character. We can be troubled if we are not sure of our belonging in the mystical body that is Christ Jesus. On the other hand, we have the power and authority to cause trouble for ourselves by taking God's promises unrealistically. No believer can out-believe God nor can God out-promise Himself. God is not a man—men are prone to lie. God's word is true and He will do whatever He says He will do.

God chose us. We are His elect, and He has given us an anointing. So wherever we are sent we can be productive in such a way that will serve as a testimony to others, for they will recognize the necessity of an anointed insight in order for us to be fruitful where others have failed. We cause the ground to yield and deliver whatever we need because of who we are in Christ Jesus. In verses 18–19 of today's scripture passage Isaac's servants dug in the valley and found a well of fresh water, although many wells had been stopped up. Hudson Taylor said, "Many Christians estimate difficulties in light of their own resources and thus attempt little and often fail in the little they attempt. All God's giants have been weak men who did great things for God because the reckoned on His power and presence with them."[31] This can be true for us when our effort and attention are in the right place.

When our focus is on *what* is going on around us (such as other dry wells) and not *who* dwells within us, we will hesitate from stepping out on our anointing. As Isaac's servants dug wells, his enemies quarreled with them because they wanted to claim the wells. Doesn't this sound familiar? The enemy recognizes our anointing and attempts to stop us from digging. But although disputes and hostility abounded, Isaac's servants continued to dig and named every well (dry or not) to show ownership. Neither Isaac nor his servants allowed their faith to be hindered, but instead by whatever means necessary, even digging well after well, they accomplished God's purpose. All of the deserted areas they touched yielded what they needed even though their enemies claimed them as their own.

God commands us to work the ground and not let it work us.

How do we know when we are making progress? We know when God tells us to work a barren area and it becomes fruitful because of the anointing He has placed on our lives. Satan does not want us to find living water in the place where God has sent us to dwell, and it does not matter how angry he becomes while we are digging. We must dwell in that area until God leads us somewhere else. Everywhere we go we will leave behind evidence that we as God's anointed lived there. God commands us to work the ground and not let it work us. Our job is to keep digging until God produces in us the strength we need for the next area He will place us. Each time we move we will get higher when the ground gets harder. As we dig down, we are going up.

Whatever Isaac touched prospered. When we are obedient the same holds true for us, not because of who we are but because of who God is. Isaac and his servants dug wells in dry land and that gave them a claim to that land. Remember, we are not alone. God is working the same ground we are working. If we dig deeper in His Word, dig deeper in our worship, and dig deeper in our praise, the living waters of God will sustain us. We will be able to claim the land where God has us digging and dwell there in joyful peace until He moves us to different ground.

A SHEEP'S REQUEST

Heavenly Father, thank You for the anointing you have placed on my life. My help comes from You and my strength lies in You. Lord, even when the winds of life blow and I am faced with opposition, help me to stand firm on my faith and dig deeper into You! I am grateful for the living waters that sustain me even when it seems as if the land is dry and hard beneath me. I know You will not leave me to work the ground alone. Amen.

TURNING BACK IS NOT THE WAY FORWARD

"You shall therefore be careful to do the commandment and the statutes and the rules that I command you today" (v. 11).

(Deuteronomy 7:1–22)

"The most pathetic person in the world
is someone who has sight,
but has no vision."
— Helen Keller[32]

Day 24

THE TABLE TALK

God wants us to know Him and follow Him in faith. Too often, however, we neglect our study of the Word and prayer and become disgruntled, questioning God's leading. This cracks the door for unbelief to enter in. A lack of faith will magnify our difficulties and make our efforts to resolve them fruitless. We yearn for the way things once were because we are unable to see what God has in store for us. A.W. Pink once commented that God is omniscient, omnipotent, can anticipate anything, and execute everything He has planned for us.[32] Despite our doubts, He knows exactly where He is taking us, but the enemy intends to discourage and trick us into believing we had it better in the past.

Even during their exodus from Egypt, the Israelites wanted to return to the land of their enslavement. They left a life of endless hard labor and had witnessed a series of miracles when they escaped, but when the first trial came upon them they became bitter and murmured against Moses. Time and time again, God supplied Israel's needs by providing water, manna, quail, and many other things, but they remained in a slave mindset. After experiencing God's providence, they continued to miss the lesson God was trying to show them—that He was trustworthy and had something better prepared for them. They were actually willing to sacrifice their freedom and return to being slaves.

You may ask, why would they want to return to bondage? Well, how different are we today? How often is this the case for us? The story of the Israelites in Numbers was written in part that we may learn from their failures. The same attitudes, reactions, tendencies, and weaknesses reside in us. When we permit the Word of God and prayer to lose their charm and become mechanical, our eyes begin to wander back to the past. We forget, as the Israelites did, that we were slaves to the enemy. Often we allow ourselves to become stuck between what is behind us and what lies before us. We crave what we left behind and pine for our past. We allow ourselves to become paralyzed by looking back, rendering us powerless to move forward. We quickly succumb to the idea that what once was were the "good old days." Human beings have an innate fear of the unknown. When God is trying to move us forward we are not always sure that we want to go. In those times, we tell God we doubt whether we can trust Him and that we feel more comfortable trusting ourselves and our past.

We allow ourselves to become paralyzed by looking back, rendering us powerless to move forward.

Fellow saints, we must keep our eyes on the prize! We cannot let the enemy have us trade in our spotless future for our dirty past. The goal of evil is to have us yearning to go back, replace, and dismiss here, now, and tomorrow with there, then, and yesterday. Turning back is to turn our back on the One who knows us. Lack of faith tells us to go back to where we think it is safe, but faith tells us to go forward to where God is working. Mistrust and skepticism will make the light burdens seem heavy, but faith makes the great burdens light.

Let us move forward with boldness and not retreat back to our comfort zone. God wants to accomplish some things in our lives, but we must be willing to follow the Holy Spirit. God's purpose for our lives is greater than we can imagine or grasp. We will never fully realize God's plan for us if we are not willing to walk forward by faith and not by sight. We serve a God of the impossible. By His supernatural power we can witness the fulfillment of His promises. God promised us the victory, and we can't advance if we retreat!

A SHEEP'S REQUEST

Heavenly Father, deliver me from the yearning to go back—away from Your love and strength. Thank You for liberating me from my past and bringing me into a bright future in You. Help me remain focused on the here, now, and tomorrow that I may experience victory in Christ Jesus. Holy Spirit, help me to not get stuck in the middle but to continue to press forward into my brighter future! Amen.

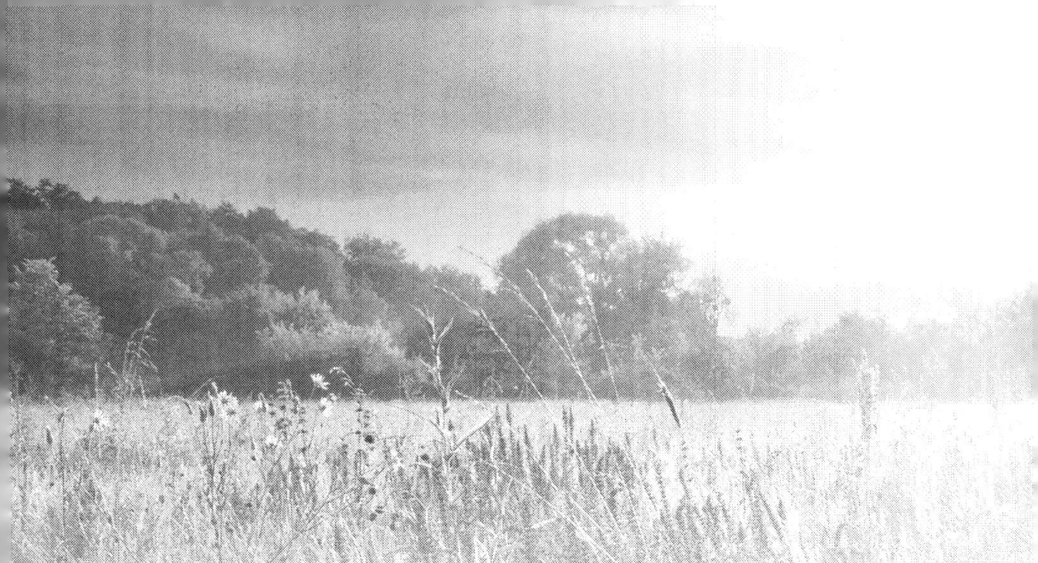

LORD, YOU HANDLE IT!

"Then Peter came up and said to him, 'Lord, how often will my brother sin against me, and I forgive him? As many as seven times?' Jesus said to him, 'I do not say to you seven times, but seventy-seven times.'"
(Matthew 18:21–22)

"The most miserable prison in the world is the prison we make for ourselves when we refuse to show mercy. Our thoughts become shackled, our emotions are chained, the will is almost paralyzed. But when we show mercy, all of these bonds are broken, and we enter into a joyful liberty that frees us to share God's love with others."
— Warren W. Wiersbe[34]

Day 25

THE TABLE TALK

Have you ever noticed how easy it can be to hold onto something done against us, but we want something that is held over us to be released quickly? We usually assess whether we want to release someone based upon the depth and intensity of the wrong committed toward us. We question the person's sincerity when requesting forgiveness. Our job, however, is not to evaluate them. We should take someone's request for pardon at face value and assume best intentions. If not, we will find ourselves withholding forgiveness, which will only breed anger and bitterness in our hearts and eventually bloom into resentment. It is impossible to be bitter and become better at the same time. Our lack of forgiveness causes us to have a disposition of constant unhappiness that only magnifies the offenses and trains the mind to incessant uneasiness.

Offenses are bound to happen, but we should not allow ourselves to become bound to those offenses. One thing we will never escape in life is the opportunity to be offended or hurt by others. It is best to resolve that we will not lose our peace over someone's sin against us. For if we perpetually ponder the pain and not the grace of God, then the corrupt nature will grow and thirst for retaliation.

If someone repents and asks for forgiveness, we must forgive them. In fact, we are commanded to forgive that same person over and over again (Luke 17:3–4). When we respond in our flesh to a person's desire to be exonerated, we give our mutual enemy a foothold into our hearts that will turn eventually into a stronghold. The purpose of forgiveness is freedom, and it behooves us to embrace Jesus's command. Otherwise, we become a prisoner to our own inability to forgive.

Forgiveness heals us, and most importantly, if we don't forgive others God will not forgive us.

Although we may often say we are unable to forgive, the reality is that we are unwilling to forgive. If we are honest with ourselves, sometimes we want to see our offender suffer or feel the same hurt we feel. Sometimes we enjoy playing the victim and may even plot revenge, but none of these tactics will make us feel any better. Instead, it is incumbent upon us to bear with integrity unjust accusations and undeserved pain in order to be an example of Jesus to others. Forgiveness heals us, and most importantly, if we don't forgive others God will not forgive us. If we allow lack of forgiveness to set in, we are assuming that the sins of others are more serious than our own sins against God.

Our focus should not be to forgive while expecting our offender to respond appropriately, but we forgive to stop the cycle of involvement. In forgiveness, we release ourselves because unforgiveness tarnishes our fellowship with the Lord. Think about it. God pardons our sins based solely on His grace, not our actions. We must allow the cross to change our perspective and realize that no sins committed against us can measure up to the innumerable sins we have committed against Christ. When we understand how egregious our sins are and how much God has forgiven us, we will find it easier to forgive others.

We all know it is difficult to let go, to release the pain and the person, but we must do so to move on. Forgiveness does not mean the offender will not suffer consequences, but we must leave it in God's hands to mediate justice. It is important also to keep at the forefront of our minds what the Bible teaches us in Romans 8:28, "For those who love God all things work together for good, for those who are called according to his purpose." God can and will take our most hurtful encounters and make something beautiful out of them.

In our passage today we see how Jesus had just finished a lesson on how to handle offense, and the disciples could still not see how greatness began with humility. Peter asked how often he should forgive one who repeatedly sinned against him, and Jesus's reply was not by any means about forgiving a bunch of times. He was telling them to forgive even in their hardest situations, even when their enemies hurt them repeatedly. Christ knew how harboring unforgiveness in our hearts would affect them. He wanted them to see how, in the grand scheme of things, the Father continually forgives us of great debts.

Forgiveness in the Greek means "to let go, leave alone or release." It doesn't mean denying the evil that was done, pretending it never happened, or glossing over the pain suffered. It does not mean that we condone the offense or will let others continually abuse us. It simply means that you are releasing the offender in order to release yourself to maintain uninterrupted fellowship with Christ. As one writer stated, "I am surrendering my rights to hurt you for hurting me." We can't hold on to it! We must release it!

A SHEEP'S REQUEST

Heavenly Father, thank You for forgiving me of my sin. I pray that You give me strength and teach me how to forgive others. Help me to love them the way You do. I pray that I can relinquish the anger and pain that I am experiencing so that I can walk in the fruit of the Spirit. Help me to heal from the hurt and release any bitterness that I may be harboring in my heart. Amen.

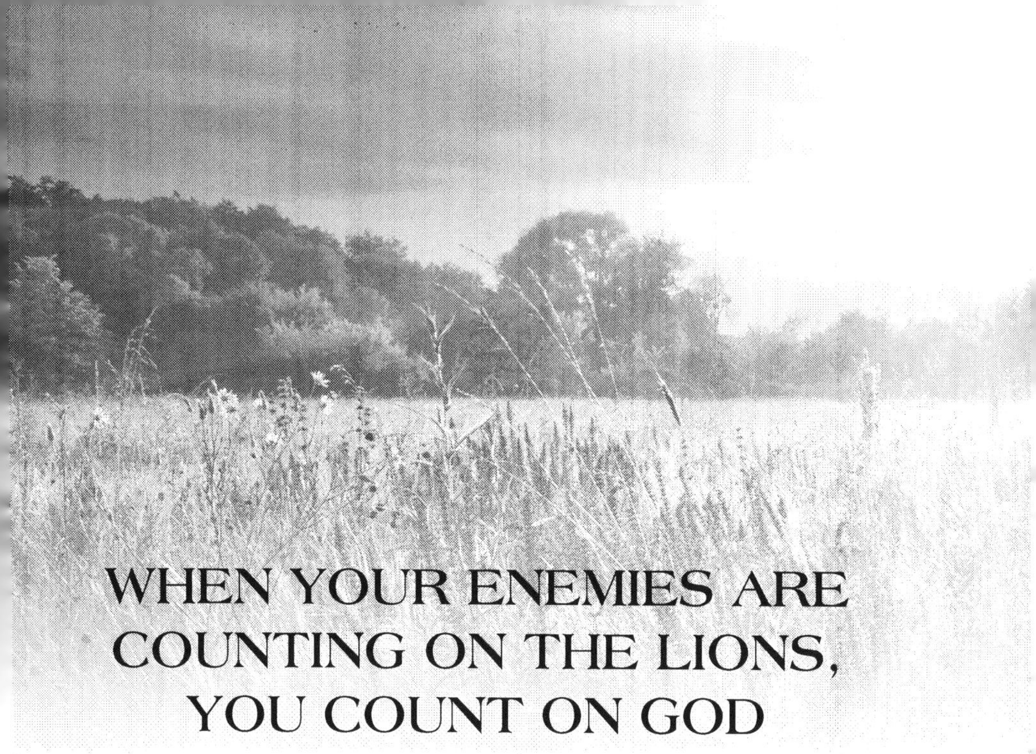

WHEN YOUR ENEMIES ARE COUNTING ON THE LIONS, YOU COUNT ON GOD

"When Daniel knew that the document had been signed, he went to his house where he had windows in his upper chamber open toward Jerusalem. He got down on his knees three times a day and prayed and gave thanks before his God, as he had done previously" (v. 10).
(Daniel 6:1–10)

"There is nothing—no circumstance, no trouble, no testing—that can ever touch me until, first of all, it has gone past God and past Christ right through to me. If it has come that far, it has come with a great purpose, which I may not understand at the moment."
— Alan Redpath[35]

Day 26

THE TABLE TALK

One thing believers know for sure is that no one has more power than the Lord for He is all powerful. The Bible proclaims undeniably that the heavens declare His glory. All of nature attests to what He can do. God can create things out of nothing, and He holds all things together. This knowledge leads us to an unavoidable question: why doesn't God use His power the way we think He should? We can name conflicts and issues that He could stop from happening, but sometimes He allows them to continue and reach destructive conclusions.

This issue is often debated as theodicy, wherein humans try to reconcile why a God who is all good would allow bad things to happen to innocent people. We believe that God can make every blind eye see, every lame person walk, and heal all of those who are sick. In many cases He does not do any of this. God is able to keep tragedies from happening; still they occur. Because God does not use His power as we often believe He should, we interpret His non-action as absence or a lack of concern.

Sometimes God will immediately come to our rescue, and other times He will allow our strength to run out in order to reveal His sufficiency.

If we entertain this kind of thinking, it will shake our confidence in God's power. We will start to wonder if He indeed has enough power to handle our situations. We come to feel as if we are fighting against God. Other questions may arise, such as, "If

He loved me and had all power, why would He put me in this position? Is the cause worth the cost? Did God launch an attack against me?" Lingering on such questions will cause us to miss what God gives when He takes something away. Sometimes God will immediately come to our rescue, and other times He will allow our strength to run out in order to reveal His sufficiency. He does not always pull us out of our situation, but He comes into our situation. That's why the Lord tells us to hide ourselves in Him, so that when the enemy attacks, he must first come through our Father. God filters every trial before it reaches us. The enemy has limits; he cannot go any further than the Lord allows.

Our safety is assured when we are near to God, not when we are far from our enemies. Circumstances don't matter with God because without God, one can never have any peace. Contrarily, one can be in the worst of circumstances with God and never lack peace. Remember this: as a child of God our character is not forged in the moment of adversity; instead our character is revealed in that moment. Sometimes when the enemy hurls an attack it is not solely toward us, but for others as well; those who would make it because we kept going and endured the trial. How we endure challenges and affects those around us.

We may feel like the Israelites who spend decades in captive exile, apparently abandoned to suffer through our trials alone. Daniel's message in today's passage emphasized God's sovereignty. He wanted to comfort the people with the assurance that despite appearances to the contrary, God was still in control. After all, Daniel found himself in a situation where his enemies had devised a plan for his destruction. He was known for faithfully serving the King but most of all for his faithfulness to the Lord. Out of jealousy, the high officials attacked him. How amazing it is to witness the degree to which some people will go in order to prevent someone from advancing.

Because we serve an all-powerful God, He is always working

things together for our good. Sometimes His plan to promote us will ride on our enemies' plot. He will use them to transport us to the next level. They may think they are pushing us out, but when God is involved they are pulling us in. So don't resist the elevation because it's not about the enemy but about the next promotion that God has for you. We should keep in mind that a thief will not waste his time breaking into an empty house, so when we are under attack there must be something valuable inside of us. The blessing of the righteous can stir up the jealousy of the wicked, just as it did in Daniel's case. We are to continue to stay right when we have been wronged and remain seated so that the Lord can bring down our enemies to make them our footstool.

Daniel never let them stop him from praying, despite knowing of a fatal punishment; we too must have that kind of resolve. If prayer got us in, then prayer will get us out. Daniel did not change in response to his enemies or the king. He did what he always did. He opened his window, prayed, and gave thanks. The enemy can't read your mind, but he can read your actions. Daniel did not just start to pray when adversity began, but he kept praying as was his usual practice. His prayer was not a response or reaction to the actions being done to him but a continuation of his commitment. He refused to concede.

We must not treat prayer as a spare wheel to be used only in case of emergency. We should always pray. Daniel was well aware that the Lord was his salvation and that his rescue rested solely in the Lord's hands. He focused on prayer to be covered constantly, not just to survive the night when put in company with lions. How we refer to God in prayer determines what we believe about Him. If we find we do not have much to say, then we may not believe much. Once we realize God is in control, we realize we are not in a place through a series of circumstances, but we are where we are for God's purpose, just like Daniel. The lions were in *Daniel's den*. We too can shut our enemies' mouths by knowing God before we get thrown into the den of adversity. Bear in mind they expect us to give up and not pray when faced with life's trials. So pray, continue in your commitment to the Lord, remember that He is all powerful, and count on Him alone to come to your rescue!

A SHEEP'S REQUEST

Heavenly Father, thank You for being an all-wise, all-knowing, and all-powerful God. I renew my commitment to seek and trust You in every situation I face in life. Lord, I declare that You are a healer, a way-maker, and my protector, peace, and joy. I believe You are working all things together for my good, and I will trust that You will come to my rescue right on time. Lord, I am counting on You and You alone as I expectantly wait for my promotion to the next level You have prepared for me. In Jesus's matchless, mighty, and powerful name, Amen.

WHEN FAITH IS ATTACKED BY DOUBT

"Now Thomas, one of the twelve, called the Twin,
was not with them when Jesus came.
So the other disciples told him, 'We have seen the Lord.'
But he said to them, 'Unless I see in his hands the mark of the nails, and place my finger into the mark of the nails, and place my hand into his side, I will never believe.'" (vv. 24–25)
(John 20:24–29)

"Doubting does not prove that a man has no faith, but only that his faith is small. And even when our faith is small, the Lord is ready to help us."
— J. C. Ryle[36]

Day 27

THE TABLE TALK

Every believer in Christ will at some point question their faith. We see many examples in the Bible of great men and women of God who doubted. Even Abraham, who was commonly known as the "father of faith" and who possessed immense faith in God, doubted the Lord regarding his ability to have a child in his old age (Genesis 17:17). Life offers to all a share of tragedies and heartaches that beget opportunities for us to doubt our faith.

Doubt manifests itself in two ways. One way is a rising disquiet that contradicts our understanding and shuts down the faith we had built up. The other way is a result of uncertainty about how things will turn out. Doubt finds its way into our thoughts because of a change in pattern or some unexpected occurrence, yet God bids us to keep believing in spite of the unsettlement.

In order for us to serve the Lord we must be willing to commit ourselves to the Word of God. We must believe the Word and act upon it, no matter what our circumstances look like in the moment. Certainly, doubt will attack our faith, but the onus is on us to not feed it or allow it permission to remain. Our response is of paramount importance to our spiritual growth. We must learn to transform those times of confusion into opportunities for our faith to mature. Our charge is to either seek out answers to our doubts or to combat them with God's absolute truth, for this is the foundation of our faith. Elisabeth Elliott stated it so profoundly, "Don't dig up in doubt what you planted in faith."[37] Doubt comes to challenge our faith, and if we allow it to linger it only grows bigger.

As some would suppose, doubt is not the opposite of faith. Disbelief is the opposite of faith. Doubt is actually part of faith because the very notion that we have doubts is evidence that we have faith. Our doubting does not shake or move God. In fact, God welcomes our questions as long as we seek to get answers based on biblical truths. Thomas, who was one of the twelve disciples, is a perfect example of someone with doubts. He earned the nickname "Doubting Thomas" for his skepticism about the resurrection. Along with the other disciples, he walked with Jesus and heard Him say He would be resurrected in three days, but he refused to believe his friends when they said they had seen the resurrected Christ. Thomas wanted to see Jesus for himself, and even went further by saying he needed to touch the wounds on His body. Jesus loved him so much He allowed him to see His hands and touch His side before urging him to stop doubting and believe. The Lord has a way of finding a sincere heart in spite of locked doors. He knew that in spite of Thomas's doubts, his heart wanted to know the Lord.

"Don't dig up in doubt what you planted in faith"
— Elisabeth Elliot

Jesus loves us just as much as He loved Thomas. He only entreats us to trust Him with our doubts and not look for natural answers to things that can only be answered spiritually. His desire to reveal Himself to us is always greater than our desire to find out more about Him. Are we willing to wrestle with God as Jacob did, leaving with a limp into the truth? Or do we attach strings to our faith? Do we tell the Lord we will believe if He does this or that first? We must not create our own obstacles to faith by expecting to have a particular feeling or experience verified before we will believe. We must obey God's Word and walk by faith and not by sight.

Augustine said, "Faith is to believe what we do not see, and the reward of this faith is to see what we believe."[38] This is the true test of our faith. When we have questions our first line of defense is to begin with what we already know to be true based on the Word of God. We wrestle with our questions until our seeds of doubt are replaced with new seeds of faith. Our raw, authentic doubts create the pathway for God's power to be revealed. When our faith is under attack by doubt, God will grant what is necessary and set up the conditions to move us into faith, just as He did for Thomas and countless others!

A SHEEP'S REQUEST

Heavenly Father, thank You for loving me and understanding that at times I have doubts and questions. I believe and trust Your Word, Lord. I praise You for Your grace and mercy that allows me with a sincere heart to ask questions about things I don't understand. Lord, I pray when my faith is under attack by doubt and it seems as if I will be consumed, that You will help me to remember the truths found in Your Word. Give me the strength and wisdom to cast down any thoughts or feelings that don't line up with Your Word. I pray my faith increases as I strive to seek You more. Amen.

I AM CONVINCED!

"Then what if you were to see the Son of Man ascending to where he was before? It is the Spirit who gives life; the flesh is no help at all. The words that I have spoken to you are spirit and life" (vv. 62–63).
(John 6:60–71)

"We are able to persevere only because God works within us, with our free wills. And because God is at work in us, we are certain to persevere. The decrees of God concerning election are immutable. They do not change, because he does not change. All whom he justifies he glorifies. None of the elect is ever lost."
— R.C. Sproul[39]

Day 28

THE TABLE TALK

It is troubling how many Christians still grapple with a basic understanding of who we are in Christ. When we have to be reminded daily and persuaded of God's love for us continuously, we deprive ourselves of experiencing the fullness of victory in Jesus. This speaks to how some have bought into the cross of Jesus but not His resurrection, which limits their ability to grow in intimacy with God. What parameters have we set in our lives that keep us stuck?

We must hunger for closeness with our Lord. Just as any relationship will not grow unless it is cultivated, so our spiritual maturity will not happen automatically. It is our responsibility to live lives marked by a hunger for intimacy with the Lord and a lifestyle that pleases Him. God will go to great lengths to show us He loves us, but how far are we willing to go to show Him we love and desire to know Him deeply? God will disclose Himself to us in very personal ways when we are open to hearing His voice.

D.L. Moody said, "God sends no one away empty except those who are full of themselves."[40] Talking is a revelation of the talker, and when God speaks His words are given for us to believe, not question. His words are life, designed to quicken and reassure us. Too often, we spend more time asking God how it is going to happen instead of centering on who said it would happen. Some things in our lives remain inactive, sitting on the shelf simply because we do not believe. The Bible teaches us we must believe in

God "and that he is a rewarder of them that diligently seek him" (Heb. 11:6 KJV). We must know the words of the Lord and be convinced of what He has said, so that when the enemy comes to counterfeit His deeds, we will not be moved.

God will disclose Himself to us in very personal ways when we are open to hearing His voice.

Many are stimulated by motives of a carnal character as opposed to being actuated by the moving of the Spirit of God in their lives. In our flesh, we easily become distracted and deceived during those seasons where God's deeds seem to cease—when He seems to be silent. He can be maddeningly difficult to understand. We encounter seasons when we feel God's power in overwhelming ways and clearly see our prayers being answered. We also encounter times of unrelenting darkness, when chaos abounds and God seems hidden. We cry out to Him in despair, as Job did when he asked why God only stood by, ignoring his desperate cries for help. During these seasons we are tempted to vacillate between what we know and what we can see.

Deductions and losses not only reveal those who do not believe but also show true believers. Brundage said, "He who is almost persuaded is almost saved and to be almost saved is to be entirely lost."[41] In these seasons of darkness we must pensively consider whether we have enough of the Word in us to be able to stand. If we are not convinced of what we believe and who God is, we begin to find ourselves making decisions based on what we used to be rather than who we desire to become. It is difficult for the Lord to quench the thirst of one who is still drinking from the past. When the mind is doubled or the heart divided, time will compel us to act according to our deepest and strongest motives. This is why we must be rooted in the infallibility of Scripture. When we feel forsaken by God, just as Job, David, and countless others did, we must remind ourselves it is simply a feeling of how we perceive things at that time, but not the reality. We must trust His promises, not our perceptions, so that we can truly stand and say, "I am convinced!"

A SHEEP'S REQUEST

Heavenly Father, thank You for Your promises telling I am never alone or forsaken. Forgive me for those times when my fears and perceptions have caused me to doubt that You love me and will see me through. Today, I declare I will stand on Your promises and remain convinced You are God and Your Word is true! Amen.

WHEN IT SITS AT THE TIP OF THE TONGUE

"Let your speech always be gracious, seasoned with salt, so that you may know how you ought to answer each person."
(Colossians 4:6)

"All men will be Peters in their bragging tongue,
and most men will be Peters in their base denial;
but few men will be Peters in their quick repentance."
— Owen Feltham[42]

Day 29

THE TABLE TALK

Words have power! God created everything using His very words, and since we were made in His image, then certainly our words have some power as well. Once we release words from our mouth, there is no taking them back. When we speak untruthful or hurtful words, the damage is done and we have displeased God. The Bible tells us we will be held accountable for the words we speak, which is why it is important for us to think before we speak.

People listen to what we say, sometimes carefully, and will often use our words to examine our lifestyle. Not only do our words influence others and how they think of us, but the words we speak also have a significant impact on our own lives. The Bible tells us our tongue has the power of life and death (Proverbs 18:21). Do we want the words from our mouths to be filled with life or death? We must carefully consider the ramifications our words have on others and ourselves.

Many fail to realize they are where they are today as a result of the words spoken yesterday and even in our distant past. Words spoken are a result of what fills our hearts. Let's ask ourselves, have we been asking for trouble with our own words and opening doors in our lives that should be closed? Too often we think we have to say something about everything and later wonder if what we said was worth anything. It would behoove us to take note that the tongue is the most responsible member of the body. As children of God we must learn the discipline of knowing what and what not to say as well as when and when not to speak.

Many fail to realize that they are where they are today as a result of the words spoken yesterday.

The enemy constantly tries to bombard our minds with evil thoughts of doubt, fear, and discouragement, which influences our speech and prevents us from receiving what God has said to us. The Bible speaks to us about thoughts, imaginations, and strongholds because once a thought comes to our mind, we must decide what to do with it. If we continue to dwell on a negative or untruthful thought, it can turn into an imagination; if the wrong thoughts are imagined for too long, they turn into strongholds, controlling our words and actions. This is why Paul in 2 Corinthians 10:5 implores us to cast down imaginations that exalt themselves above the truth of God. He tells us to "take every thought captive to obey Christ."

The enemy wants us to respond quickly when a thought comes to mind so we will bring harm to ourselves. Great wisdom is required in order for us to avoid this temptation to speak rashly. Let the Holy Spirit guide us in determining when to speak. When He gives us something to say, continue to seek Him for the right time to say it. Both substance and timing are important.

Silence puzzles people. They hear silence and begin to wonder what is wrong. They may go restless; however, silence is the natural context from which we listen and speak. One who is being taught and lead by the Holy Spirit does not waste valuable time but instead becomes valuable in time. Satan will try to cause a miscarriage of God's plans by urging us to speak when we should be silent and silent when we should speak. If we don't know how to be silent, we won't know how to speak.

There is a duty in silence such as when God told the children of Israel to not be afraid, but to stand still and see the salvation of the Lord. Sometimes He will call us to silence to see His works and other times to hear His works. Silence can teach us things we will never learn if we are speaking. We must learn to exercise what I like to call "sanctified silence," keeping silent until I can speak under control, which is exactly what God requires of us. Our ability to control our tongues measures our maturity. Plato said, "Wise men speak because they have something to say and fools speak because they have to say something."[43]

The ministry of the tongue is communicating in silence and speech. Isaiah 53:7 says Jesus was "oppressed," "afflicted," and "yet he opened not his mouth," even when all our iniquities were laid upon Him. His death was never a capitulation to weakness, but an exercise of deliberate control. He kept silent while Satan began to pile up the accusations against you and me. When He spoke, He spoke with authority. Let us use Jesus as our perfect example for how to control our tongues.

A SHEEP'S REQUEST

Heavenly Father, thank You for Your Word, for teaching me that I am able to watch what I say, and to know when to speak. Lord, give me discipline over my tongue and help me to choose words that speak life and not death. I pray God that You will take control when words that are not pleasing to You sit at the tip of my tongue. Amen.

THE PRESSURE OF PRIDE

"So to keep me from becoming conceited because of the
surpassing greatness of the revelations,
a thorn was given me in the flesh, a messenger of Satan
to harass me, to keep me from becoming conceited." (v. 7)
(2 Corinthians 12:1–10)

"God sends no one away empty
except those who are full of themselves."
— D. L. Moody[44]

Day 30

THE TABLE TALK

Many times during our sanctification by the Holy Spirit we raise a rebuttal. We naturally strain against the process of what the Lord seeks to do in our lives because we don't think much work needs to be done. This mindset births the self-defining thought that all of God's work for us is addition because nothing needs to be subtracted. This kind of prideful attitude cripples our spiritual growth, and it normally goes undetected for a period of time. We learn how to keep the clay container clean while the content on the inside is constantly deteriorating. As a matter of fact, pride is one of the few things that can grow in the human heart without any sustenance. Most of us do not walk around trumpeting our awesomeness. We just feed upon it inwardly. God wants to drain off our tanks of pride. Augustine said, "Thou must be emptied of that wherewith thou art full that thou mayest be filled with that whereof thou art empty."[45] Could this be why God is working on areas in our life that we feel do not require any work? Interestingly enough, the areas where we do not think need any work turn out to be the very areas that are holding us back from our full potential in the Lord.

Only God knows the swelling effect that comes from His deposited word in us and amazing work on us. If we ignore Him, then we will believe the illusion we are competent to run our own lives, and that will only destroy us. Satan knows man has no reference point by which to define himself apart from God. If he can get us to switch the mirror of humility to the decorated bling-bling view of a powerful person who rarely needs help, then he has us right where he wants us. He has us wrapped up in our own prideful ways, and this is what leads to every other vice in our lives. In order to combat our pride, we must humble ourselves under the mighty hand of our Lord and Savior. The only true way to be humble is to recognize at the peak of our pride that we are nothing without God. "For I say, through the grace given unto me, to every man that is among you, not to think of himself more highly than he ought to think; but to think soberly," (Romans 12:3 KJV) meaning don't overestimate ourselves or hold too high opinions about our own abilities. He teaches us that in order to change the direction of our thinking we must think of ourselves in a realistic way. We should not lift ourselves up to a position that could only be held by God. Holding onto our pride causes us to disregard the presence of God. Just when we think we don't have pride is the ideal time to recognize we have much of it. We must recognize the smallest evil, if neglected, will reach the greatest magnitude.

Only God knows the swelling effect that comes from His deposited word in us and amazing work on us.

The apostle Paul painted a picture about the pressure of pride where he explained that if he did not have insight, he might be tempted to exalt himself. He was a world traveler and a public speaker, often bedazzling those who listened to him, yet he refused to be captured by the pressure of pride. We too, like Paul, must be aware of the danger pride will cause. It will cause us to filter out the issues seen in ourselves and also to filter out the goodness seen in others. When we become defensive because of a challenge or rebuke, our temper often gets us in trouble, and then pride keeps us there. Pride will make us desperate for attention, respect, and worship. It causes us to neglect others, prefer some people over others, seek people with power, and neglect those we consider weak, unattractive, and inconvenient. Then when pride is at its crowning, we will engage in blame-shifting and self-justification. Before we realize it, pride has consumed us and taken a seat in the very center of our lives.

Pride will take us to places we never intended to go. It does not like accountability or submitting to the sovereignty of God. Sometimes the enemy will have us so focused on silencing our critics that we will offset God's purpose for our present position. If Satan can have us feeling embarrassed, we will focus on off-setting "haters" and start exaggerating our testimony. We will move from hearing from heaven and doing God's assigned work to doing our own work and wanting heaven to hear about it.

The only replacement for pride is repentance. If we cannot repent for the trespasses we have committed against God, then we are engaging in what is called "ego tripping." Our hearts must first and foremost desire to be seen and understood on the basis of our service to God and others. "Though if I should wish to boast, I would not be a fool, for I would be speaking the truth; but I refrain from it, so that no one may think more of me than he sees in me or hears from me" (2 Corinthians 12:6). The question is not whether we can survive our failures but whether we can survive our successes. Everything we have is because God is our source, and we must never presume that we can make it in life by our own strength and effort.

A SHEEP'S REQUEST

Heavenly Father, forgive me for allowing pride to exist in my life. I pray You search my heart and cleanse me from all of my sins for I know pride is at the root of every sin. Help me not to think more highly of myself than I ought to and to not think of others as inconveniences. Without You Lord, I am nothing. All that I am and all that I have is because of You. Amen.

IT'S BEHIND ME NOW

"And as they brought them out, one said,
'Escape for your life. Do not look back or stop anywhere
in the valley. Escape to the hills,
lest you be swept away'" (v. 17).
(Genesis 19:15–25)

"A great leader's courage to fulfill his vision
comes from passion, not position."
— John C. Maxwell[46]

Day 31

THE TABLE TALK

The Lord has an impeccable way of showing us how far off our focus is from where it should be. We often fight the perfect plan of God to embrace that which could destroy us. How many times have we asked God to remove something from our lives, and when He honors our request we look back and wonder what happened to the very thing we wanted gone? A fight with our flesh might ensue as we try to keep from turning back, telling ourselves to move forward because we already know what's behind us. Why is it we readily surrender those things we are tired of, but we fight to hold on to the things God is tired of? It is in those times that we begin to realize the intensity of our flesh, and at the same time the Lord's love for us is revealed all the more as He works to release us from what has hindered our walk with Him. We must stop staring at our past! If it was part of God's will for our lives, He would allow us to see it head on.

Our lives change when we decide to follow Jesus. Following Christ means we must leave some things behind and make Him our number one priority. Luke 5 records that when Jesus called Simon Peter and Levi the tax collector, "they left everything and followed Him" (v. 11). They dropped everything, right there on the spot. The Lord may not require us to leave everything behind, and those possessions He asks us to discard are different from person to person. He does, however, require each of us forsake anything in our life that does not honor Him. We cannot surrender halfway. We cannot serve two masters. God will not tolerate His child leading a double lifestyle.

In Luke 17 Jesus implores us to remember Lot's wife. He used her as a warning to us of what happens when we refuse to leave things behind to follow Him. God told Lot to leave his home and gave strict instruction for them not to look back, but Lot's wife had become so entangled with their accumulated treasures in Sodom that she looked back in regret of losing them. She loved those things more than she loved the Lord. Two voices were competing for her loyalty, and regrettably she yielded to the wrong voice. She looked back and was instantly turned into a pillar of salt. Lot's wife took her eyes off the path of the Lord and longed for her old world instead. When we look back we fail to see Jesus and are left to our own defenses. One must trust the Word of God implicitly, for He knows what is right and what is to come. Rebekah trusted in God and left her family to marry Isaac, becoming mother to the Israelites. How many of us would be like Lot and Rebekah, or would we be like Lot's wife?

Everyone who followed Jesus left something . . .

Satan preys on those of us who are too close to our yesterdays because we have divided hearts, which are indicators of unsurrendered will. We must place our trust in God. He sees things we are not privy to, so don't fight His plan as He is simply trying to rescue us for our own good. We can't travel this journey with God by carrying excess baggage. He will show us what we need and what we must leave behind. Everyone who followed Jesus left something, and the same must hold true for us. What is God asking you to leave behind? Remember, in God, it's not what we have to leave, but what we have left! Now that we have heard God's call to follow Him, we must not linger in our old ways, lest their pull overpowers us and draw us back to them. Let us choose wisely and decisively, declaring it is all behind us now and pledge to never take a backward glance.

A SHEEP'S REQUEST

Heavenly Father, give me strength to surrender those things that stand in the way of my loyalty to You. I submit to You and desire to obey Your will for my life. Reveal to me anything I am holding onto that I need to leave behind in order to move forward in You! Amen.

Sources

1 F.B. Meyer, AZQuotes.com, Wind and Fly LTD, 2018, https://www.azquotes.com/quote/544772, (November 14, 2018).

2 Thomas Merton, AZQuotes.com, Wind and Fly LTD, 2018, https://www.azquotes.com/quote/570781, (November 14, 2018).

3 Arthur W. Pink, AZQuotes.com, Wind and Fly LTD, 2018, https://www.azquotes.com/quote/565672 (November 16, 2018).

4 Erwin Lutzer, Sermonindex.net, http://www.sermonindex.net/modules/articles/index.php?view=article&aid=30573 (November 17, 2018).

5 Philip Yancey. AZQuotes.com, Wind and Fly LTD, 2018. https://www.azquotes.com/quote/865007, (November 16, 2018).

6 C. S. Lewis. AZQuotes.com, Wind and Fly LTD, 2018. https://www.azquotes.com/quote/369698, (November 16, 2018).

7 John. R. Rice, *Hindrances to Prayer,* Jesus-Is-Savior.com. http://www.jesus-is-savior.com/Books,%20Tracts%20&%20Preaching/Printed%20Books/Dr%20John%20Rice/Hindrances/h_03.htm, (November 26, 2018).

8 John Calvin, AZQuotes.com, Wind and Fly LTD, 2018,

https://www.azquotes.com/quote/45687 (November 16, 2018).

9 Helen Keller, AZQuotes.com, Wind and Fly LTD, 2018, https://www.azquotes.com/quote/866621 (November 19, 2018).

10 Augustine of Hippo, AZQuotes.com, Wind and Fly LTD, 2018, https://www.azquotes.com/quote/662102, (November 16, 2018).

11 Augustine of Hippo, AZQuotes.com, Wind and Fly LTD, 2018, https://www.azquotes.com/quote/12955, (November 16, 2018).

12 Alexander MacLaren., AZQuotes.com, Wind and Fly LTD, 2018, https://www.azquotes.com/quote/662636 (November 16, 2018).

13 John Flavel, AZQuotes.com, Wind and Fly LTD, 2018, https://www.azquotes.com/quote/662460, (November 21, 2018).

14 Thomas á Kempis, *Of the Imitation of Christ* (London: T. Nelson and Sons, 1888), 34.

15 Toby Powers, "The Sheep Of His Pasture," Outreach Web Properties: https://www.sermoncentral.com/sermons/the-sheep-of-his-pasture-toby-powers-sermon-on-men-s-day-90243 (November 15, 2018).

16 William Secker, *The Consistent Christian*, http://www.gracegems.org/29/secker.htm (November 16, 2018).

17 Charles Spurgeon. AZQuotes.com, Wind and Fly LTD, 2018. https://www.azquotes.com/quote/280428, (November 16, 2018).

18 Smith Wigglesworth. AZQuotes.com, Wind and Fly LTD, 2018. https://www.azquotes.com/quote/1421165, (November 16, 2018).

19 A. W. Tozer. AZQuotes.com, Wind and Fly LTD, 2018. https://www.azquotes.com/quote/560624, (November 16, 2018).

20 Charles Spurgeon, AZQuotes.com, Wind and Fly LTD, 2018, https://www.azquotes.com/quote/867548, (November 16, 2018).

21 Jim Elliot, AZQuotes.com, Wind and Fly LTD, 2018, https://www.azquotes.com/quote/347269, (November 16, 2018).

22 Matthew Henry, "Nehemiah," *Commentary on the Whole Bible,* Christian Classics Ethereal Library, http://www.ccel.org/ccel/henry/mhc2.Neh.ix.html, (November 16, 2018).

23 Henry Ward Beecher, AZQuotes.com, Wind and Fly LTD, 2018, https://www.azquotes.com/quote/22263, (November 16, 2018).

24 A. W. Pink, The Attributes of God (Ada: Baker Books, 2006)

25 Jurgen Moltmann, "Theology of Hope," Online Journal of Public Theology, http://pubtheo.com/theologians/moltmann/theology-of-hope-0b.htm (November 22, 2018).

26 A.W. Tozer, *God Tells the Man Who Cares: God Speaks to Those Who Take Time to Listen* (Chicago: Moody Bible Institute, 1993).

27 Alexander MacLaren, AZQuotes.com, Wind and Fly LTD, 2018, https://www.azquotes.com/quote/1403864, (November 16, 2018).

28 Augustine of Hippo, AZQuotes.com, Wind and Fly LTD, 2018, https://www.azquotes.com/quote/12931, (November 22, 2018).

29 "Continue," Merriam-Webster, https://www.merriam-webster.com/dictionary/continue, (November 22, 2018).

30 J. C. Ryle, AZQuotes.com, Wind and Fly LTD, 2018, https://www.azquotes.com/quote/868377, (November 16, 2018).

31 Hudson Taylor, AZQuotes.com, Wind and Fly LTD, 2018, https://www.azquotes.com/quote/1312170, (November 23, 2018).

32 Helen Keller, AZQuotes.com, Wind and Fly LTD, 2018, https://www.azquotes.com/quote/155043, (November 16, 2018).

33 A. W. Pink, quoted by J.I. Packer, *Knowing God* (Downers Grove: InterVarsity Press, 1973), 80.

34 Warren W. Wiersbe. AZQuotes.com, Wind and Fly LTD, 2018, https://www.azquotes.com/quote/523163, (November 16, 2018).

35 Alan Redpath, AZQuotes.com, Wind and Fly LTD, 2018, https://www.azquotes.com/quote/1107524, (November 16, 2018).

36 J. C. Ryle, AZQuotes.com, Wind and Fly LTD, 2018, https://www.azquotes.com/quote/703997, (November 16, 2018).

37 Elisabeth Elliot Gren, *Quest for Love* (Grand Rapids: Fleming H. Revell, 1996).

38 Augustine of Hippo, AZQuotes.com, Wind and Fly LTD, 2018, https://www.azquotes.com/quote/12927, (November 24, 2018).

39 R.C. Sproul, *Chosen by God* (Carol Stream, Ill.: Tyndale, 1986), 148.

40 Dwight L. Moody, AZQuotes.com, Wind and Fly LTD, 2018, https://www.azquotes.com/quote/545532, (November 24, 2018).

41 Brundage, as quoted by David West, "Almost Persuaded," Grace For All Publications, https://grace4all.com/almost-persuaded/ (November 23, 2018).

42 Owen Feltham, AZQuotes.com, Wind and Fly LTD, 2018, https://www.azquotes.com/quote/845467, (November 16, 2018).

43 Plato, as quoted by Philip Graham Ryken, ed. R. Kent Hughes, *Ecclesiastes: Why Everything Matters*, Preaching the Word (Wheaton: Crossway, 2010).

44 Dwight L. Moody, AZQuotes.com, Wind and Fly LTD, 2018, https://www.azquotes.com/quote/545532, (November 16, 2018).

45 Augustine of Hippo, *Expositions on the Book of Psalms*, 6 vols. (London: Walter Smith, 1884), 6:167.

46 John C. Maxwell, AZQuotes.com, Wind and Fly LTD, 2018, https://www.azquotes.com/quote/416188, (November 16, 2018).

32463031R00119

Made in the USA
Middletown, DE
09 January 2019